Anonymous

How to Cook

Anonymous

How to Cook

ISBN/EAN: 9783744789165

Printed in Europe, USA, Canada, Australia, Japan

Cover: Foto ©Lupo / pixelio.de

More available books at **www.hansebooks.com**

HOW TO COOK.

—o—

THE HOUSEKEEPER'S FRIEND.

—o—

CONTAINING

VALUABLE RECIPES FOR COOKING ALL KINDS OF
MEATS, FISH, OYSTERS AND GAME.

ALSO

FULL DIRECTIONS
HOW TO MAKE BREAD, CAKE,
PIES, PUDDINGS, AND ALMOST EVERY DISH
THAT IS USED IN FAMILY
COOKING.

—o—

THIS BOOK HAS BEEN CAREFULLY PREPARED BY AN OLD
AND EXPERIENCED COOK IN ONE OF OUR
LEADING RESTAURANTS.

—o—

NEW YORK:
FRANK TOUSEY, PUBLISHER,
18 ROSE STREET.

CONTENTS.

HOW TO COOK.

───o───

The Housekeeper's Friend.

───o───

SOUPS.

Ox-Tail Soup.—*Time, four hours and a half.*—Cut up two ox-tails, separating them at the joints; put them into a stew-pan with about an ounce and a half of butter, a head of celery, two onions, two turnips, and two carrots cut into slices, and a quarter of a pound of lean ham cut very thin; the pepper corns and savory herbs, and about half a pint of cold water. Stir it over a quick fire for a short time to extract the flavor of the herbs, or until the pan is covered with a glaze. Then pour in three quarts of water, skim it well, and simmer slowly for four hours, or until the tails are tender. Take them out, strain the soup, stir in a little flour to thicken it, add a glass of port wine, the catsup, and half a head of celery (previously boiled and cut into small pieces). Put the pieces of tail into the stew-pan with the strained soup. Boil it up for a few minutes, and serve. This soup can be served clear, by omitting the flour and adding to it carrots and turnips cut into fancy shapes, with a head of celery in slices. These may be boiled in a little of the soup, and put into the tureen before sending it to table.

Soup a la Julienne, or Vegetable.—Cut various kinds of vegetables in pieces, celery, carrots, turnips, onions, etc., and having put two ounces of butter in a stew-pan, put the vegetables on the top of the butter, together with any others that may be in season. Stew or fry them over a slow fire, keeping them stirred, and adding a little of the stock occasionally; soak small pieces of crust of bread in the remainder of the broth or stock, and when the vegetables are nearly stewed, add them, and warm the whole up together.

Chicken Soup.—*Time, four hours.*—Boil a pair of chickens with great care, skimming constantly, and keeping them covered with water. When tender, take out the chicken and remove every bone from the meat; put a large lump of butter into a frying-pan, and dredge the chicken meat well with flour; lay in the hot pan; fry a nice brown, and keep it hot and dry. Take a pint of the chicken water, and stir in two large spoonfuls of curry powder, two of butter, and one of flour, one teaspoonful of salt and a little cayenne; stir until smooth, then mix it with the broth in the pot; when well mixed, simmer five minutes, then add the browned chicken. Serve with rice.

MACARONI SOUP.—*Time, three-quarters of an hour.*—The macaroni must be boiled in water for ten minutes, strained and put into boiling stock, in the proportion of half a pound to the gallon; simmer slowly for half an hour, and serve very hot, with grated cheese on a separate dish.

CLAM CHOWDER.—Twenty-five clams chopped fine, six potatoes, chopped fine, two onions chopped fine, a piece of salt pork, also chopped, and butter about the size of an egg; salt and pepper to taste; the clam juice and one pint of milk and the same of water; six crackers rolled, one nutmeg grated, teaspoonful celery-seed. Boil these slowly for at least four hours, adding water if it becomes too thick; half an hour before serving add coffee cupful of tomato catsup and two tablespoonfuls of Worcestershire sauce. When ready for table add tumbler of sherry; cut a lemon in slices and serve with it.

BEEF BROTH.—Take a leg of beef, cut it in pieces; put it into a gallon of water; skim it; put in two or three blades of mace, some parsley, and a crust of bread; boil it till the beef and sinews are tender. Toast bread and cut into dice; put it in a dish; lay in the beef, and pour on the broth.

KIDNEY SOUP.—*Time, six hours.*—Add to the liquor from a boiled leg of mutton a bullock's kidney, put it over the fire, and when half done, take out the kidney, and cut it into pieces the size of dice. Add three sticks of celery, three or four turnips, and the same of carrots, all cut small, and a bunch of sweet herbs, tied together. Season to your taste with pepper and salt. Let it boil slowly for five or six hours, adding the catsup. When done, take out the herbs, and serve the vegetables in the soup. It is always better (as all soups are) made the day before it is wanted.

OYSTER SOUP.—Take 2 quarts of oysters and drain them with a fork from their liquor; wash them in one water to free them from grit; cut in small pieces 2 slices of lean bacon, strain the oyster liquor and put in it the bacon, oysters, some parsley, thyme, and onions tied in a bunch as thick as the thumb, season with pepper and salt, if necessary; let it boil slowly, and when almost done, add a lump of butter as large as a hen's egg, rolled in flour, and a gill of good cream. It will take from 20 to 30 minutes to cook it.

CLAM SOUP.—*Time, one hour.*—25 clams, opened, raw and chopped fine; add 3 quarts of water; boil them one half hour, then add a pint of milk, 1 onion chopped fine, thicken with butter and flour; beat 3 eggs in the tureen and pour your broth over them boiling hot.

ROAST MEATS.

ROAST BEEF.—The sirloin or rib is considered the best piece for roasting. After selecting the piece to roast, place it in the dripping-pan, with some salt and water; put it in the oven, which should be kept good and hot; baste it now and then with the drippings from the meat. A piece of 8 pounds will take from 1½ to 2 hours to roast. When almost done, sprinkle the meat with salt.

ROAST VENISON.—A haunch of buck will take 3½ or 3¾ hours roasting; doe, only 3¼ hours. Venison should be rather under than overdone.

Spread a sheet of white paper with butter, and put it over the fat, first sprinkling it with a little salt; then lay a coarse paste on strong paper, and cover the haunch; tie it with fine pack-thread, and set it at a distance from the fire, which must be a good one. Baste it often; ten minutes before serving, take off the paste, draw the meat nearer the fire, and baste it with butter and a good deal of flour, to make it froth up well.

Gravy for it should be put into a boat, and not into the dish, (unless the venison has none), and made thus: Cut off the fat from two or three pounds of a loin of old mutton, and set it in steaks on a gridiron for a few minutes, just to brown one side; put them into a sauce-pan with a quart of water, cover close for an hour, and simmer it gently; then uncover it, and stew till the gravy is reduced to a pint. Season with only salt.

Currant-jelly sauce must be served in a boat.

TO ROAST PORK.—Pork requires a longer time in roasting than any of the preceding meats. When stuffing is to be used, it must be composed of chopped sage and onion, pepper and salt. The pieces should be neatly and well scored in regular stripes on the outer skin, to enable the carver to cut slices easily. Before putting to the fire, rub the skin with salad oil, to prevent its blistering, and baste very frequently. The basting may be done by rubbing it with a piece of butter in a muslin bag, when there is not enough of dripping. The gravy for pork may be the same as for other joints, hot water and salt poured over it on the dish. It is considered an improvement to have apple-sauce served in a small tureen, as it assists in overcoming the richness or lusciousness of the meat, and imparts a slight acidulous flavor.

ROAST SHOULDER OF MUTTON.—*Time, a quarter of an hour to each pound.*—Take out the bone and fill the space with a stuffing made of bread crumbs, salt pork chopped fine, pepper, salt and sage, or sweet marjoram.

STUFFED LEG OF MUTTON.—Boil two large white onions until tender, then chop fine; add breadcrumbs and sage to taste, a little salt and pepper; then slit the sinewy part of the leg and insert the stuffing, and roast.

To Roast Veal.—The best parts of veal for roasting are the fillet, the breast, the loin, and the shoulder. The fillet and the breast should be stuffed, particularly the fillet; the stuffing to be composed of crumbs of bread, chopped suet and parsley, a little lemon peel, and pepper and salt, wet with an egg and a little milk. The piece should have a slow fire at first, and will require longer time to dress than beef or mutton. Let it be well basted with butter when there is not sufficient dripping from the joint. The gravy for roast veal is either the usual hot water and salt, or thin melted butter, poured over the meat.

To Bake Ham.—*Time, four hours.*—Take a medium-sized ham and place it to soak for ten or twelve hours. Then cut away the rusty part from underneath, wipe it dry, and cover it rather thickly over with a paste of flour and water. Put it into an earthen dish, and set it in a moderately-heated oven for four hours. When done, take off the crust carefully and peel off the skin; put a frill of cut paper around the knuckle, and raspings of bread over the fat of the ham, or serve it glazed and garnished with cut vegetables.

Pig's Head Baked.—Let it be divided and thoroughly cleaned; take out the brains, trim the snout and ears, bake it an hour and a half, wash the brains thoroughly; blanch them, beat them up with an egg, pepper and salt, and some finely-chopped or pounded sage, and a small piece of butter; fry or brown them before the fire; serve with the head.

Beef Heart.—Let it be thoroughly well boiled, and the skin removed. Wipe it dry with a clean cloth, stuff it with veal stuffing; roast two hours and a quarter. Make a brown gravy, as for hare; and serve with the gravy and currant jelly.

The most pleasant way to the palate of dressing this dish, is to roast the heart rather less than two hours; let it get cold, cut it in pieces and jug it the same as hare.

———o———

STEWED MEATS.

Stewed Shin of Beef.—Saw the bone into three or four pieces, put them into a stew-pan, and *just* cover them with cold water. When the pot simmers, skim it clean, and then add the sweet herbs, one large onion, celery, twelve black peppercorns, and twelve allspice. Stew it very gently over a slow fire till the meat is tender. Then peel the carrots and turnips, and cut them into shapes; boil them with twelve small button onions till tender. The turnips and onions will take a quarter of an hour to boil, the carrots *half* an hour. Drain them carefully.

Beef Stewed With Onions.—Cut 2 pounds of tender beef into small pieces, and season with pepper and salt; slice one or two onions and add to it, with water enough to make a gravy.

Let it stew slowly till the beef is thoroughly cooked; then add some pieces of butter rolled in flour, enough to make a rich gravy. Cold beef may be cooked in the same way, but the onions must then be cooked before adding them to the meat. Add more boiling water if it dries too fast.

AN ENGLISH STEW OF COLD ROAST BEEF.—*Time, fifteen minutes.*—Cut the meat in small and rather thin slices, season them highly with salt and pepper, and dip each lightly in bread-crumbs moistened in gravy or melted butter. Dress them neatly on a dish, and lay over them a thin layer of cut pickles, and moisten the whole with a glassful of pickled vinegar and the preserved gravy of the roast beef; heat in a Dutch oven, and garnish with fried sippets or potato balls.

LOIN OF MUTTON STEWED.—Remove the skin, bone it, and then roll it; put it in a stewpan with a pint and a half of water, 2 dessert-spoonfuls of pyroligneous acid, a piece of butter, sweet herbs, and an onion or two; when it has stewed nearly four hours, strain the gravy, add 2 spoonfuls of red wine, heat up and serve with jelly sauce.

IRISH STEW.—*Time, two hours and a half.*—Put 2 pounds of mutton cutlets or chops, and 4 pounds good potatoes, peeled and sliced, in alternate layers in a large saucepan or stewpan, season to taste with pepper and salt, and a finely-shred onion; add a pint of cold water, and simmer gently for two hours. Serve very hot.

TO BOIL A HAM.—Well soak the ham in a large quantity of water for twenty-four hours; then trim and scrape it very clean, put it into a large stewpan with more than sufficient water to cover it; put in a blade of mace, a few cloves, a sprig of thyme and two bay leaves. Boil it for four or five hours, according to its weight; and when done, let it become cold in the liquor in which it was boiled. Then remove the rind carefully without injuring the fat; press a cloth over it to absorb as much of the grease as possible, and shake some bread-raspings over the fat, or brush it thickly over with glaze. Serve it cold, garnished with parsley, or aspic jelly in the dish. Ornament the knuckle with a paper frill and vegetable flowers.

BOILED BULLOCK'S HEAD.—*Time to boil, five hours.*—This is a good dish for a large family. Place the head in salt water for six hours, to cleanse it; then wash and remove the palates, and place them again in salt and water; put the head in a saucepan, with sufficient water to cover; boil for five hours, adding 2 carrots, 2 turnips, and 2 onions, cut small; when done remove the head from the soup, and remove the bone from the meat; serve soup and meat in tureen; the palates, when white, boiled until tender, then pressed until cold, make a delicious relish for lunch or supper.

PIG'S HEAD BOILED.—This is a more profitable dish, though not so pleasant to the palate, It should first be salted, which is usually done by the pork butcher. It should be boiled 1 1-4 hours; it must be boiled gently, or the meat will be hard.

POTTED VEAL.—This may be potted as beef, or thus: Pound cold veal in a mortar, work up with it in a powder, mace, pepper and salt; shred the leanest part of tongue very finely, or ham is sometimes used; place in a jar or pot a layer of the pounded veal, and upon that a layer of the tongue, and continue alternately until the pot is full, seeing that every layer is well pressed down; pour over the top melted clarified butter. If it is desired, and which is frequently done, to marble the veal, cut the tongue or ham in square dice instead of shredding it; but care must be taken that they do not touch each other or the effect is destroyed.

TO BOIL A LEG OF MUTTON.—A leg of mutton should be kept four or five days before boiling. Before putting it into the pot, bend around the shank, cutting the tendon at the joint if necessary, so as to shorten the leg. Two hours of slow, equal boiling will be sufficient for a good-sized leg of mutton. Some persons, to make the leg look white and tasteful, wrap it tightly in a cloth in boiling; but this spoils the liquor for broth. It is not safe to boil vegetables with a leg of mutton, as they are apt to flavor the meat. Dish the leg with a little of the liquor, placing the lower side uppermost, convenient for carving. A good leg of mutton will yield sufficient gravy.

TO BOIL BEEF.—Reckon the time from the water coming to a boil. Keep the pot boiling, but let it boil *very slowly.* If you let the pot cease boiling, you will be deceived in your time; therefore watch that it does not stop, and keep up a good fire. Just before the pot boils the scum rises. Be sure to skim it off carefully, or it will fall back and adhere to the meat.

BEEF A-LA-MODE.—Remove the bone from a round, or any piece of beef that will stew well. Make a stuffing of bread crumbs seasoned with sweet marjoram, pepper, mace, nutmeg, and onions, or shalots chopped fine. Mix this together with two eggs well beaten, and add, if you like, some chopped salt pork. Fill the place from which the bone was taken with this seasoning, rubbing what is left over the outside of the meat. Bind, and skewer it well, to secure the stuffing. You may stick whole cloves into the meat here and there, or lard it with fat pork. Cover the bottom of your stewpan with slices of the ham, or salt pork, and having put in the meat, lay slices of the ham or pork over it. Pour in about a pint of water; cover the pan closely, and bake in an oven six, seven, or eight hours, according to the size of the piece. Add, if you like, a tea-cupful of port wine, and the same of mushroom catsup to the gravy; but it is very good without wine. This dish is best cold.

CALVES' TONGUES.—Wash them well, and put them in hot water for a short time, in order to take off the hard skin; lard them here and there with large pieces of bacon; put them in a saucepan, so as to yield a little gravy, with two or three large onions and carrots. When the whole is well glazed, add some water, salt, a clove, and a sprig of thyme, and let it simmer very slowly for five hours. Just before serving, skim the sauce, and thicken it with some flour; open each tongue in half, so that it forms a heart shape, and pour the sauce over, adding to it either some pickled gherkins, sliced, or some mushrooms.

To STEW KIDNEYS.—Cut the kidneys into slices, wash them and dry them with a clean cloth, dust them with flour, and fry them with butter until they are brown. Pour some hot water or beef gravy into the pan, a few minced onions, pepper and salt, according to taste, and add a spoonful or two of mushroom catsup before dishing. Minced herbs are considered an improvement to many tastes; cook slowly ten or fifteen minutes.

——o——

BROILED AND FRIED MEATS.

STEAKS—BROILED.—They should not be cut more than three quarters of an inch thick, or they will not be done well through. Let the gridiron be perfectly clean, and heat and grease it before laying on the meat. Set it over a bed of clear bright coals, and when done on one side turn the steaks with tongs made for the purpose, or a knife and fork. In a quarter of an hour they will be well done; or if you like them rare, ten or twelve minutes will be sufficient. Pour off into a dish and save all the gravy that accumulates while boiling; and when done lay the steaks in a dish, and season to your taste with pepper, salt, and butter. Serve hot.

To FRY BEEF-STEAKS.—Cut the steaks as for broiling, and on being put into the pan, shift and turn them frequently. Let them be done brown all over, and placed in a hot dish when finished. Gravy may be made by pouring a little hot water into the pan after the steaks are out and the fat poured away, with a little pepper, salt, catsup, and flour. The gravy so formed is to be poured into the dish with the steaks. Serve to table immediately.

To FRY PORK CHOPS.—Pork chops should be cut rather thin, and be thoroughly dressed. They may be either simply fried in the same manner as chops, or fried after being dipped in egg, and sprinkled with crumbs of bread, and sage and onion finely chopped. No gravy is expected with pork chops. If any sauce be used, it must be apple sauce.

To FRY PORK SAUSAGES.—All sausages are fried alike, and require to be dressed very slowly. Before being put into the pan, they should be pricked in several places with a fine fork, to prevent their bursting by the expansion of the air within.

It is common in England to bring fried sausages to table neatly laid out on a flat dish of mashed potatoes. The sausages and potatoes are helped together. They may also be laid in links on toasted bread, and garnished with poached eggs around the dish.

Fried sausages are sometimes used for garnishing roast turkey.

To Fry Lamb Steaks.—Dip each piece into well-beaten egg, cover with bread crumbs or corn meal, and fry in butter or new lard. Serve with mashed potatoes and boiled rice. Thicken the gravy with flour and butter, adding a little lemon juice, and pour it hot upon the steaks, and place the rice in spoonfuls around the dish to garnish it.

Calf's Liver and Bacon.—Soak two or three livers in cold water for half an hour, then dry it in a cloth, and cut it into thin, narrow slices; take about a pound of bacon, or as much as you may require, and cut an equal number of thin slices as you have of liver: fry the bacon *lightly*, take it out and keep it hot; then fry the liver in the same pan. seasoning it with pepper and salt, and dredge over it a little flour. When it is a nice brown, arrange it around the dish with a roll of bacon between each slice. Pour off the fat from the pan, put in about two ounces of butter well rubbed in flour to thicken the gravy; squeeze in the juice of a lemon and add a cupful of hot water; boil it and pour it into the center of the dish. Serve it garnished with forcemeat balls or slices of lemon.

Veal Cutlets.—*Time, twelve to fifteen minutes.*—Let the cutlet be about half an inch thick, and cut it into pieces the size and shape of a crown piece. Chop some sweet herbs very fine; mix them well with the bread crumbs. Brush the cutlets over with the yolk of an egg, then cover them with the bread crumbs and chopped herbs; fry them lightly in butter, turning them when required. - Take them out when done.

Mix about an ounce of fresh butter with the grated peel of half a lemon, a little nutmeg, and flour; pour a little water into the frying-pan, and stir the butter, flour, and grated lemon peel into it; then put the cutlets into this gravy to heat. Serve them piled in the center of the dish with thin rolls of bacon as a garnish.

Veal Cutlets with Fine Herbs.—Melt a piece of butter in the frying-pan; put in the cutlets with salt, pepper, and some spice; move them about in the butter for five minutes: have ready some mixed herbs and mushrooms chopped finely; sprinkle half over one side of the cutlets, and, when fried enough, turn and sprinkle them with the other half; finish frying, and add the juice of a lemon; set them around the dish with the seasoning in the center.

Pork Chops.—Cut the chops about half an inch thick, and trim them neatly; put a frying-pan on the fire, with a bit of butter: as soon as it is hot, put in your chops, turning them often till brown all over: a few minutes before they are done, season with powdered sage, pepper and salt.

Ham and Eggs.—Chop finely some cold boiled ham, fat and lean together, say a pound to four eggs; put a piece of butter in the pan, then the ham; let it get well warmed through, then beat the eggs light; stir them in briskly.

POTTED OX-TONGUE.—Cut about a pound and a half from an unsmoked boiled tongue; remove the rind. Pound it in a mortar as fine as possible with six ounces butter and a small spoonful each of mace, nutmeg, and cloves beaten fine. When perfectly pounded, and the spice well blended with the meat, press it into small potting-pans and pour clarified butter over the top. A little roast veal added to the potted tongue is an improvement.

TRIPE.—Must be washed in warm water, and cut into squares of three inches; take one egg, three tablespoonfuls of flour, a little salt, and make a thick batter by adding milk; fry out some slices of pork, dip the tripe into the batter, and fry a light brown.

BEEF STEAK SMOTHERED WITH ONIONS.—Cut up six onions very fine; put them in a saucepan with two cupfuls of hot water, about two ounces of good butter, some pepper and salt; dredge in flour. Let it stew until the onions are quite soft, then have the steak broiled, put into the saucepan with the onions; then simmer about ten minutes, and send to the table very hot.

———o———

MEAT PIES.

BEEFSTEAK PIE.—A good common paste for meat pies, and which is intended to be eaten, is made as follows: Three ounces of butter and one pound of flour will be sufficient for one dish. Rub the butter well among the flour, so as to incorporate them thoroughly. If the butter be fresh, add a little salt. Mix up the flour and butter with as much cold water as will make a thick paste. Knead it quickly on a board, and roll it out flat with a rolling-pin. Turn the dish upside down upon the flattened paste, and cut or shape out the piece required for the cover. Roll out the parings, and cut them into strips. Wet the edges of the dish, and place these strips neatly around on the edges, as a foundation for the cover. Then take some slices of tender beef, mixed with fat; those from the rump are the best. Season them with pepper and salt,, and roll each slice up in a small bundle, or lay them flat in the dish. Put in a little gravy or cold water, and a little flour for thickening. Then, after putting in the meat, lay the cover on the dish, pressing down the edges closely to keep all tight. If any paste remains, cut or stamp it into ornaments, such as leaves, and place these as a decoration on the cover.

MUTTON PIE.—Strip the meat from the bones of a loin of mutton without dividing it, and cut it into nice, thin slices, and season them with pepper and salt; put a pie-crust around the edge of a pie-dish, place in it a layer of mutton, then one of forcemeat, and again the slices of mutton, with three or four halves of kidneys, at equal distances; then pour in a gravy made from the bones, seasoned and well cleared from fat. Moisten the edge with water. Cover with a paste half an inch thick; press it around with your thumbs, make a hole in the center, and cut the edges close to the dish; ornament the top and border according to your own taste, and bake it.

CHESHIRE PORK PIE.—Take the skin and fat from a loin of pork, and cut it into thin steaks; season them with pepper, salt, and nutmeg; line a pie-dish with puff-paste, put in a layer of pork, then of pippins, pared and cored, and about two ounces of sugar; then place in another layer of pork, and half a pint of white wine, and lay some butter on the top; cover it over with puff-paste, pass a knife through the top to leave an opening, cut the paste even with the dish, egg it once, and bake it.

VEAL PIE.—Take about two pounds of veal from the loin, fillet, or any odd pieces you may have. Parboil enough to clear it of the scum. If it is to be done in a pot, make a very light paste according to directions for such purposes; roll it out rather thick; and having your pot well greased, lay it around the sides, cutting out pieces to prevent thick folds, as the circle diminishes. Put in a layer of meat, with salt and pepper. Enrich with butter, or slices of salt pork, and dredge in a little flour. So proceed until you have put all in. Cover with paste, and cut a hole in the top for the escape of the steam. Pour in a portion of the water in which the meat was boiled. Set it over a slow fire; watch that it does not burn; and if it get too dry, add more of the same water, through the hole in the top. If you wish the crust brown, cover the top with a heater or bake-pan cover. It will be done in an hour and a half.

If the pie is *baked*, make a richer crust, in the proportion of a pound of butter to two pounds of flour; put it in a pan, in the same manner as above; notch the edges of the paste handsomely, and bake about the same time.

———o———

HASH.

HASH.—Take cold pieces of beef that have been left over, and chop them fine; then add cold boiled potatoes chopped fine; add pepper and salt and a little warm water; put all in a frying-pan and cook slowly for twenty minutes.

MUTTON HASHED.—Cut the remains of a cold leg or shoulder of mutton into thin slices, whether fat or lean; flour and pepper well and leave on the dish. Boil the bones, well broken up, with a few onions minced well, add some salt, a little mushroom catsup and the hashed meat; warm over a slow fire, but do not let it boil; then add port wine and currant jelly, or omit, as you please. If the former, it will impart a venison flavor; if the latter method is adopted it will be plain.

———o———

MISCELLANEOUS MEATS.

BOLOGNA SAUSAGES.—Take three pounds of lean beef, the same of lean pork, two pounds of fat bacon, and a pound and a half of beef suet; put the lean meat into a stewpan of hot water, and set it over the fire for half an hour, then cut it small, each sort by itself, shred the suet, and bacon or ham, each by itself. Season with pepper, thyme chopped fine, and ground mace; fill ox skins with it, tie them in lengths, and put them in a beef brine for ten days; then smoke them the same as ham or tongue. Rub ground ginger or pepper over the outside after they are smoked, and keep them in a cool, dry place.

MINCED VEAL.—Cut cold veal as fine as possible, but do not chop it. Put to it a very little lemon peel shred, two grates of nutmeg, some salt, and four or five spoonfuls of either a little weak broth, milk, or water; simmer these gently with the meat, but take care not to let it boil, and add a bit of butter rubbed in flour. Put sippets of thin toasted bread, cut into a three-cornered shape, around the dish.

MINT SAUCE FOR ROAST LAMB.—Two table-spoonfuls of chopped green mint; one tablespoonful of pounded sugar, and a quarter of a pint of vinegar. Pick and wash the green mint very clean, chop it fine, mix the sugar and vinegar in a sauce tureen, put in the mint, and let it stand.

———o———

POULTRY, GAME, ETC.

TO ROAST A TURKEY.—Pluck the bird carefully, and singe off the down with lighted paper; break the leg bone close to the foot and hang up the bird and draw out the strings from the thigh. Never cut the breast; make a slit down the back of the neck and take out the crop that way. then cut the neck bone close, and after the bird is stuffed the skin can be turned over the back and the crop will look full and round. Cut around the vent, making the opening as small as possible, and draw carefully, taking care that the gall-bag and the gut joining the gizzard are not broken. Open the gizzard and remove the contents, and detach the liver from the gall-bladder. The liver, gizzard and heart, if used in the gravy, will need to be boiled an hour and a half, and chopped as fine as possible. Wash the turkey and wipe thoroughly dry, inside and out; then fill the inside with stuffing, and either sew the skin of the neck over the back, or fasten it with a small skewer. Sew up the opening at the vent; then run a long skewer into the pinion and thigh, through the body, passing it through the opposite pinion and thigh. Put a skewer in the small part of the leg, close on the outside of the sidesman, and push it through. Pass a string over the points of the skewers, and tie it securely at the back.

To Roast Partridges.—Pick, draw, singe and clean them the same as fowls. Make a slit in the neck and draw out the craw: twist the neck around the wing and bring the head around to the side of the breast. The legs and wings are trussed the same as fowls, only the feet are left on and crossed over one another. Put them down to a clear fire and baste well with butter. When about half done, dust a little flour over them; let them be nicely browned. They will require to roast from twenty minutes to half an hour each. Serve on toasted bread dipped in the gravy, with gravy and bread-sauce.

Roast Chicken.—Draw, singe, and truss the chicken and put it between some slices of bacon; take care to tie up the legs on the spit, so that they be kept firm; baste it with its own gravy; when done to a point, (*i. e.* half an hour), serve with cresses around it, seasoned with vinegar and salt.

Stewed Duck with Green Peas.—Put a deep stewpan on the fire with a piece of fresh butter; singe the duck; flour it, and put it in the stewpan to brown, turning it two or three times; pour out the fat, but let the duck remain in the pan; put to it a pint of good gravy, a pint of peas, two lettuces cut small, a bundle of sweet herbs, and a little pepper and salt; cover close, and let them stew half an hour. Give the pan a shake now and then. When they are just done, grate in a little nutmeg and a little beaten mace, and thicken it with a piece of butter rolled in flour; shake it all together for a few minutes; then take out the sweet herbs, lay the duck in a dish, and pour the sauce over it. Garnish with mint, chopped fine.

Chicken Fricassee.—Half boil a chicken in a little water; let it cool, then cut it up, and simmer in a gravy made of some of the water in which it was boiled, and the neck, head, feet, liver, and gizzard stewed well together. Add an onion, a faggot of herbs, pepper and salt, and thicken with butter rolled in flour added to the strained liquor with some nutmeg, then give it a boil, and add a pint of cream; stir over the fire, but do not let it boil. Put the hot chicken into a dish, pour the sauce over it, add some fried forcemeat balls, and garnish with slices of lemon.

Chicken Jelly.—Boil a pair of chickens until you can pull the meat from the bones; remove all the meat and allow the bones to boil about half an hour longer; stand this in a cool place and it will become jellied; the next day cut the meat into small pieces, melt the jelly, and throw it in; then add two tablespoonfuls of Worcestershire sauce, two of walnut sauce, one tablespoonful of salt, a pinch of powdered mace, cloves and allspice, slice ten hard-boiled eggs and two lemons; line a large bowl or form with these slices, then pour in the mixture and let it stand in a cool place, but not to freeze. The water should just cover the chickens when put to boil. This is a very ornamental dish, and keeps for a long time.

Stuffing for Turkey.—Mix thoroughly a quart of stale bread, (very finely grated), the grated rind of a lemon, quarter of an ounce of minced parsley and thyme (one part thyme, two parts parsley), and pepper and salt to season. Add to these one unbeaten egg and half a cup of butter; mix all well together, and moisten with hot water or milk. Other herbs than parsley or thyme may be used, if preferred, and a little onion, finely minced, added if desired.

SAGE AND ONION STUFFING, for Geese, Ducks, or Pork.— Wash, peel and boil three onions in two waters, to extract the strong flavor, and scald eight sage leaves for a few minutes. Chop the onions and leaves very fine, mix them with five ounces of bread crumbs, seasoned with pepper and salt, a piece of butter broken into pieces, and the yolk of one egg.

To ROAST WILD FOWL.—The flavor is best preserved without stuffing. Put pepper, salt and a piece of butter into each. Wild fowl require much less dressing than tame. A rich, brown gravy should be sent in the dish; and when the breast is cut into slices, before taking off the bone, a squeeze of lemon, with pepper and salt, is a great improvement to the flavor. To take off the fishy taste which wild fowl sometimes have, put an onion, salt and hot water into the dripping-pan and baste them for the first ten minutes with this; then take away the pan and baste constantly with butter.

PRAIRIE CHICKENS.—Skin the chickens, which makes them sweeter; cut them open on the back and through the breast. Fry them in butter, with salt and-pepper to the taste. Cook them to a nice brown.

CHICKEN CROQUETTES.—One large chicken, two sweetbreads, wine-glass of cream, one loaf baker's stale bread. Cook chicken and sweet-bread separately, saving the chicken broth. Chop chicken, meat, and sweet-bread finely together, season with pepper, salt, parsley, and half a teaspoonful grated onion. Rub the bread into crumbs until you have equal quantities of crumbs and meat. Place over the fire as much of the chicken broth as will moisten well the crumbs, into which stir the cream, and butter size of an egg. When it boils, stir in the crumbs until they adhere to the spoon. Add meat, and, when cold, two well-beaten eggs. Mold into rolls, with your hands, roll them in crumbs, and fry in hot lard, like doughnuts.

To ROAST DUCKS.—Pick, draw, and singe them. Cut off the head, and dip the feet in boiling water, to remove the yellow skin; truss them plump, turning the feet flat upon the back. Stuff the same as goose, and serve with gravy and apple-sauce. An hour will roast a duck. Green peas usually accompany roast duck.

To BOIL A TURKEY.—A boiled turkey is a most delicate and excellent dish, and requires to be dressed with extreme care. Clean the turkey from feathers and stumps, and singe off the hairs, taking care not to blacken the skin. Draw, and wipe it inside with a clean, dry cloth; cut off the legs at the first joint; draw out the sinews; then pull down the skin and push the legs inside; cut the head off close to the body, leaving the skin long, and draw out the craw. Make a good veal-stuffing, and put it into the breast, leaving sufficient room for the stuffing to swell; then draw the skin of the breast over the opening, and sew it neatly across the back, so that when the turkey is brought to table no sewing will appear. Place the gizzard in one wing, and the liver in the other; turn the wings on the back, and fasten them to the sides.

GAME PIE.—*Time, to bake, about two hours.*—"Raise" a crust to a size corresponding with the quantity of your game. Cut with a sharp knife the flesh from the best parts; keep each kind separate, and set them aside for a moment. Then split the heads, break the bones, and put them with the inferior parts into a stewpan, with a roasted onion, a carrot, a tea-spoonful of salt, twenty black peppercorns, sprigs of winter savory, marjoram, lemon, and common thyme, two bay leaves, half a clove of garlic, and half a pound of gravy beef. Stew in a very little water (according to the quantity of the meat) five hours. When done, skim and strain and set it aside to cool. Line the whole of your raised crust with a thin layer of short paste, then a layer of fat bacon or ham cut in thin slices. Now put in your different kinds of game in layers, not round, but from the bottom, filling up the corners and crevices with forcemeat stuffing. Having mixed together two teaspoonfuls of cayenne, and half a grated nutmeg, sprinkle a little of them over each layer. Finish the filling with a layer of ham or bacon; put over it a layer of the short paste; then cover with the raised crust. Pinch around the sides, ornament by crimping leaves set according to fancy, and bake in a moderate oven an hour, an hour and a half, or two hours, according to size. When both pie and gravy are nearly cold, put the point of a funnel into the small hole, (which, by the way, you must make in the top of the pie before you bake it), and gently pour through it the gravy you prepared.

To STEW RABBITS.—Wash the rabbits well; cut them in pieces, and put them in to scald for a few minutes. Melt a piece of butter, in which fry or brown the rabbits for a short time. When slightly browned, dust in some flour; then add as much gravy or hot water as will make sufficient soup. Put in onions, catsup, pepper and salt, according to taste. Stew for an hour slowly.

———o———

FISH.

BROILED SALMON.—*Time, ten to fifteen minutes.*—Cut slices of an inch, or an inch and a half thick from the middle of a large salmon; dust a little Cayenne pepper over them; wrap them in oiled or buttered paper, and broil them over a clear fire, first rubbing the bars of the gridiron with suet. Broiled salmon is extremely rich, and really requires no sauce. The slices may also be simply dried in a cloth, floured, and broiled over a clear fire; but they require the greatest care then to prevent them from burning. The gridiron is always rubbed with suet first.

To Pickle Salmon.—Remove the bone from a boiled salmon, or part of one that has been boiled, and lay it in a dish; boil a sufficient quantity of the liquor the fish was boiled in, with the same quantity of vinegar; one ounce of black pepper, one ounce of allspice, four bay leaves, and some salt. When cold, pour it over the fish; and in twelve or fourteen hours it will be fit for use.

Salmon—To Boil.—This fish cannot be too soon cooked after being caught; it should be put into a kettle with plenty of cold water and a handful of salt—the addition of a small quantity of vinegar will add to the firmness of the fish—let it boil gently; if four pounds of salmon, fifty minutes will suffice; if thick, a few minutes more may be allowed.

The best criterion for ascertaining whether it be done, is to pass a knife between the bone and the fish—if it separates readily, it is done; this should be tried in the thickest part; when cooked, lay it on the fish-strainer transversely across the kettle, so that the fish, while draining, may be kept hot. Place a fish-plate upon the dish on which the salmon is to be served, fold a clean white napkin, lay it upon the fish-plate, and place the salmon upon the napkin. Garnish with parsley.

Broiled Mackerel.—Prepare by boiling a short time a little fennel, parsley and mint; when done take it from the fire and chop all together fine, mix a piece of butter with it, a dust of flour, pepper and salt; cut your fish down the back and fill it with this stuffing; oil your gridiron and oil your fish; broil then over a clear slow fire.

To Cook Shad-roes.—First, partially boil them in a small covered pan, and then fry in hot lard, after covering or sprinkling with flour.

Fried Eels.—*Time, eighteen or twenty minutes*—Prepare and wash the eels, wipe them thoroughly dry, and dredge over them a very little flour; if large, cut them into pieces of about four inches long, brush them over with egg, dip them in bread crumbs, and fry them in hot fat. If small, they should be curled around, and fried, being first dipped into egg and bread crumbs. Serve them up garnished with fried parsley.

To Bake a Shad, Rock-fish or Bass.—Clean the fish carefully, sprinkle it lightly with salt, and let it lie a few minutes; then wash it, season it slightly with Cayenne pepper and salt, and fry it gently a light brown. Prepare a seasoning of breadcrumbs, pounded cloves, parsley, Cayenne pepper and salt; strew it over and in the fish; let it stand an hour. Put it in a deep dish, and set it in the oven to bake; to a large fish, put in the dish, the juice of a lemon made thick with loaf sugar, one-half teacupful of tomato catsup; to a small one, allow in proportion the same ingredients; baste frequently and garnish with sliced lemon.

FRESH HALIBUT FISH-BALLS.—To two pounds of boiled halibut add double the quantity of hot mashed potatoes; the fish must be picked in small pieces; add butter the size of an egg, a teaspoonful of powdered sugar, salt, and two eggs; mix them well, make them into round flat balls, and when the weather is cold they can stand over night, but in summer they must be made in the morning. Have a kettle of boiling-hot lard, put in only a few at a time, and boil them until they are a nice light brown. If the lard is not quite boiling, they will soak the fat, and if too hot, they will come out black.

HALIBUT.—STEWED.—Put into a stewpan half a pint of fish broth, a tablespoonful of vinegar, and one of mushroom catsup, two good-sized onions cut in quarters, a bunch of sweet herbs, add one clove of garlic, and a pint and a half of water; let it stew an hour and a quarter, strain it off clear, put into it the head and shoulders of a fine halibut, and stew until tender; thicken with butter and flour and serve.

SUN FISH, FROST FISH, SMELTS, MINNOWS, or other small fish, must be well cleaned and dried, and shaken in a floured cloth, and may then be fried, either with a little butter, or in boiling fat; or they may be first dipped in egg, and sprinkled with fine bread crumbs.

They will scarcely take more than two minutes to make them of a nice brown color, when they are done. Let them be drained on a hair sieve, before the fire, till they are pretty free from fat.

TO BAKE A LARGE FISH WHOLE.—Cut off the head and split the fish down nearly to the tail; prepare a dressing of bread, butter, pepper and salt, moistened with a little water. Fill the fish with this dressing, and bind it together with fine cotton cord or tape; lay the fish on a grate, or a bake-pan, or a dripping-pan, and pour around it a little water, and melted butter. Baste frequently. A good-sized fish will bake in an hour. Serve with the gravy of the fish, drawn butter, or oyster sauce.

CHOWDER.—Take some thin pieces of pork and fry brown; cut each piece into several pieces, place them by layers in your pork fat, sprinkle a little pepper and salt—add cloves, mace, sliced onions; lay on bits of fried pork, if you choose, and crackers soaked in cold water; then turn on water just sufficient to cover them, and put on a heated bake-pan lid. After stewing about twenty minutes, take up the fish, and mix two tea-spoonfuls of flour with a little water, and stir it into the gravy, adding a little pepper and butter, catsup, and spices also, if you choose. Cod and bass make the best chowder. Clams and black-fish are tolerably good. The hard part of the clam should be cut off and rejected.

OYSTERS, CLAMS, AND SHELL-FISH,

BROILED OYSTERS.—Take the largest and finest oysters. See that your gridiron is very clean. Rub the bars with fresh butter, and set it over a clear, steady fire, entirely clear from smoke, or on a bed of bright, hot wood coals. Place the oysters on the gridiron, and when done on one side, take a fork and turn them on the other, being careful not to let them burn. Put some fresh butter in the bottom of a dish. Lay the oysters on it, and season them slightly with pepper. Send them to table hot.

SCALLOPED OYSTERS.—*Time, a quarter of an hour.*—Butter some tin scallop-shells, or, if you have not any, a small tart dish. Strew in a layer of grated bread, then put some thin slices of butter, and then oysters enough to fill your shells or dish. Cover them thickly with bread-crumbs, and again add slices of butter. Pepper the whole well, and add a little of the liquor kept from the oysters. Put butter over the whole surface, and bake in a quick oven. Serve them in their shells or in the dish.

Brown them with a salamander. If you have not one, make the kitchen shovel red-hot, and hold it over closely enough to brown your scallops.

OYSTER PIE.—Line a deep dish with fine puff paste. Lay a plate of the same size over the top, to support the upper crust, which you must lay on and bake before the oysters are put in, as in the time required for cooking the paste, the oysters would be overdone. While the paste is baking, prepare the oysters. Take their liquor, and, having strained, thicken it with the yolk of egg, either boiled hard and grated or beaten thoroughly, and a piece of butter rolled in bread-crumbs. Season with mace and nutmeg. Stew the whole for five minutes, or till well done. Carefully remove the cover from the pie; take out the plate; put in the oysters, with their gravy; replace the cover, and send to table, hot. If you like the pie dryer, put in only half the liquor. You may make flowers of strips of the paste, and garnish the crust.

TO STEW OYSTERS.—*Time, ten minutes.*—After pouring off the juice, put the oysters into some salt water, and pass each one between the thumb and finger to get rid of the slime. Then to 100 oysters add half a pound of butter rubbed up with a teaspoonful of flour; stir for ten minutes or till done, then add a half pint of cream, but do not permit it to boil, otherwise the cream will curdle; add salt and Cayenne pepper to the taste.

TO FRY OYSTERS.—Make a thick batter of eggs, milk, flour, pepper and salt, and dip the oysters singly in the batter; after which, fry them in dripping or lard in a frying-pan, being careful that they do not stick together. A sauce may be used, composed of the liquor of the oysters, thickened with flour and butter, and seasoned with Cayenne pepper and a little catsup.

LOBSTER PATTIES.—*Time, twenty minutes.*—Roll out the puff paste about a quarter of an inch thick, take a hen-lobster already boiled, pick the meat from the tail and claws, and chop it fine, put it in a stewpan with a little of the inside spawn pounded into a mortar until quite smooth, with an ounce of butter, half spoonful of cream, the same of veal gravy, essence of anchovy, lemon juice, Cayenne pepper and salt, and a tablespoonful of flour and water. Let it stew five minutes, fill the patties, and serve.

CLAM FITTERS.—Take twelve large or twenty-five small clams from their shells; if the clams are large divide them. Mix two gills of wheat flour with one gill of milk, half as much of the clam liquor, and one egg well beaten. Make the batter smooth, and then stir in the clams. Drop the batter by tablespoonfuls in boiling lard; let them fry gently, turning them when done on one side.

TO MAKE A CRAB PIE.—Procure the crabs alive, and put them in boiling water, along with some salt. Boil them for a quarter of an hour or twenty minutes, according to the size. When cold, pick the meat from the claws and body. Chop all together, and mix it with crumbs of bread, pepper and salt, and a little butter. Put all this into the shell, and brown before the fire. A crab shell will hold the meat of two crabs.

LOBSTERS TO BE COLD.—Procure the lobsters alive. Hen-lobsters are the best, as they have spawn in and about them. Put them in boiling water, along with some salt, and boil from half an hour to three-quarters of an hour, or more, according to the size. When done, take them out of the water and wipe the shells. Before they are quite cold, rub the shells with a buttered cloth. Take off the large claws, and crack the shells carefully, so as not to bruise the meat. Split the body and tail lengthwise, in two pieces. This may be done with a knife. Place the whole of the pieces ornamentally on a dish and garnish with parsley.

SOFT-SHELL CRABS.—Soft-shell crabs must be dipped in beaten egg, and then in grated bread or cracker crumbs, and thrown into a hot frying-pan in which salt pork has been fried out for the purpose; it gives them a much better flavor than butter or lard.

———o———

VEGETABLES ETC

GREEN PEAS.—A delicious vegetable, a grateful accessory to many dishes of a more substantial nature. Green peas should be sent to the table *green*; no dish looks less tempting than peas if they wear an autumnal aspect. Peas should also be young, and as short a time as possible should be allowed to elapse between the periods of shelling and boiling. If it is a matter of consequence to send them to table in perfection, these rules must be strictly observed. They should be as near of a size as a discriminating eye can arrange them; they should then be put in a colander, and some cold water suffered to run through them in order to wash them; then having the water in which they are to be boiled slightly salted and boiling rapidly, pour in the peas; keep the saucepan uncovered and keep them boiling swiftly until tender; they will take about twenty minutes, barely so long, unless older than they should be; drain completely, pour them into the tureen in which they are to be served, and in the center put a slice of butter, and when it has melted stir round the peas gently, adding pepper and salt; serve as quickly and as hot as possible.

TOMATOES FRIED.—Do not pare them, but cut in slices as an apple; dip in cracker, pounded and sifted, and fry in a little good butter.

GREEN CORN.—*Time, twenty minutes.*—This should be cooked on the same day it is gathered; it loses its sweetness in a few hours, and must be artificially supplied. Strip off the husks, pick out all the silk, and put it in boiling water; if not entirely fresh, add a tablespoonful of sugar to the water, but *no salt;* boil twenty minutes, fast, and serve, or you may cut it from the cob, put in plenty of butter and a little salt, and serve in a covered vegetable dish.

LIMA BEANS.—Shell them into cold water; let them lie half an hour or longer; put them into a saucepan with plenty of boiling water, a little salt, and cook till tender. Drain, and butter well, and pepper to taste.

STRING BEANS.—Break off both ends, and string carefully; if necessary pare both edges with a knife. Cut the beans in pieces an inch long, and put in cold water a few minutes. Drain and put them into boiling water, with a piece of bacon or salt pork. Boil quickly for half an hour, or till tender. Drain in a colander, and dish with plenty of butter.

POTATO BALLS.—Mash boiled potatoes till they are quite smooth; add a little salt, then knead them with flour to the thickness required; toast on the griddle, pricking them with a fork to prevent their blistering. Eat them warm, with fresh butter; they will be found equal to crumpets, and much more nutritious.

POTATOES MASHED WITH ONIONS.—Prepare some boiled onions by passing them through a sieve, and mix them with potatoes. Regulate the proportions according to taste.

ROASTED POTATOES.—Clean thoroughly; nick a small piece out of the skin, and roast in the oven of the range; a little butter is sometimes rubbed over the skin to make them crisp.

BOILED POTATOES.—Rather more than parboil the potatoes; pare off the skin, flour them and lay them on a gridiron over a clear fire; send them to table with cold fresh butter.

FRIED POTATOES.—Remove the peel from an uncooked potato. After it has been thoroughly washed, cut the potato into thin slices, and lay them in a pan with some fresh butter; fry gently a clear brown, lay them cne upon the other in a small dish, and send to table as an *entre mets.*

TO COOK SPINACH.—Wash and clean the spinach thoroughly from grit, then boil it in salt and water; press the water entirely out of it, and chop it as fine as powder. A quarter of an hour before serving, put it into a saucepan with a piece of butter mixed with a tablespoonful of flour and half a tumblerful of boiling water, some salt, pepper, and nutmeg, and let it simmer fifteen minutes. Serve with hard-boiled eggs on the top.

SWEET POTATOES.—They should neither be pared nor cut; but select those that are nearest of a size, to cook together. When done, pour off the water and let them steam as other potatoes. They are sometimes half boiled, then cut in slices, and fried in sweet drippings, or butter. The best way to keep them is to bury them in dry sand.
These are better roasted or baked than boiled.

TO BAKE THEM.—Wash them clean and wipe them dry; then place them in a quick oven. They will take from half an hour to an hour, according to their size.

TO ROAST THEM.—Prepare them as for baking, and either cook them in the hot ashes of a wood fire, or in a Dutch oven. They take from half to three-quarters of an hour to be done.

YOUNG BEETS BOILED.—Wash them very clean, but neither scrape nor cut them. Put them in boiling water, and, according to their size, boil them from one to two hours. Take off the skin when done, and put over them pepper, salt and a little butter. Beets are very nice baked, but require a much longer time to cook.

HOW TO BOIL CABBAGE.—Cut off the stalk and strip off the outer leaves; quarter and wash them in plenty of water, and leave them to soak, top downwards, with a little salt in the water, for an hour or two. Put them into plenty of boiling water, with a good handful of salt and a bit of soda, and boil them till the stalk feels tender. Cabbage requires boiling from twenty to forty minutes, according to size. Drain through a colander. Greens may be pressed between two plates.

TO DRESS CAULIFLOWERS.—Having picked them into small pieces, which is absolutely necessary in order to remove the slugs with which this vegetable abounds, wash it thoroughly in several waters, and let it lay to soak for half an hour before you dress it. Put it into a saucepan of boiling water, with a lump of salt, and when tender it will be done; let it drain in a colander, and serve it up with melted butter. Some persons may prefer to see them brought to table whole, but they must then take the chance of being helped, along with the cauliflower, to some unsightly insect, which would be sufficient to disgust the least delicate stomach; besides, if properly boiled, and laid carefully in the dish, the pretty appearance of the vegetable is by no means destroyed by its having been divided.

EGG PLANT.—Cut the egg plant in slices half an inch thick, and let it lay for several hours in salted water, to remove the bitter taste. To fry it put the slices in the frying-pan with a small quantity of butter, and turn them when one side is done. Be sure that they are thoroughly cooked. Stuffed egg plant is sometimes preferred to fried. Peel the plant whole, cut it in two, and let it lay in salted water. Then scoop out the inside of the plant, chop it up fine, mixing crumbs of bread, salt and butter with it; fry it, return it to the hollow egg plant—join the cut pieces together, and let them bake awhile in an oven.

ASPARAGUS.—Cut the heads about four or five inches long; scrape them and throw them into cold water; tie them in bundles; put them into boiling water with plenty of salt in it; let them come quickly to a boil—they will take from a quarter of an hour to twenty minutes. When tender take them up with a slice; drain them well; remove the string, and lay the asparagus in a dish, heads inwards, on slices of toast previously dipped in the liquor. Serve with melted butter. Sea kale is dressed in the same manner.

FRENCH OR SCARLET BEANS.—Cut off the two ends and string them, then split and cut them in two, throw them into a pan of clean water, and put them into plenty of boiling water with salt and a little soda. When they are soft, which will be in about a quarter of an hour or twenty minutes, strain them through a sieve, and serve them with melted butter in a boat.

WINTER SQUASH.—Cut it in pieces, take out the seeds and pare as thin as possible; steam or boil until soft and tender. Drain and press well, then mash with butter, pepper, salt and a very little sugar. Summer squash may be cooked the same way; if extremely tender they need not be pared.

SUCCOTASH.—*Time one hour and a half.*—Cut off the corn from the cobs, and put the cobs in just water enough to cover them, and boil one hour; then remove the cobs and put in the corn and a quart of Lima beans, and boil thirty minutes. When boiled, add some cream or milk, salt and butter.

EGGS.

To Boil Eggs.—The boiling of eggs is a very simple opera-tion, but is frequently ill-performed. The following is the best mode:—Put the egg into a pan of hot water, just off the boil. When you put in the egg, lift the pan from the fire and hold it in your hand for an instant or two. This will allow the air to es-cape from the shell, and so the egg will not be cracked in boil-ing. Set the pan on the fire again, and boil for three minutes or more, if the egg be quite fresh, or two minutes and a half, if the egg has been kept any time. Eggs to be used hard for salads and other dishes, should be put into cold water, and boiled for a quarter of an hour after the water comes to the boil. In this case, the shells should not be taken off till the eggs are cold.

To Poach Eggs.—Take a shallow saucepan or frying-pan, and fill it about half full of water. Let the water be perfectly clean, not a particle of dust or dirt upon it. Put some salt in-to the water. Break each egg into a separate tea-cup, and slip it gently from the cup into the water. There is a knack in do-ing this without causing the egg to spread or become ragged. A good way consists in allowing a little water to enter the cup and get below the egg, which sets the egg to a certain extent, before it is allowed to lie freely in the water. If the water be about boiling point, one minute is sufficient to dress the egg, but the eye is the best guide; the yolk must retain its liquid state.

Omelettes.—Omelettes are composed of eggs, and anything that the fancy may direct to flavor and enrich them. For a common omelette, take six eggs, and beat them well with a fork in a basin; add a little salt..Next take a little finely-chop-ped parsley, finely-chopped eschalot or onion, and two ounces of butter cut into small pieces, and mix all this with the egg. Set a frying-pan on the fire with a piece of butter in it; as soon as the butter is melted, pour in the omelette, and continue to stir it till it assumes the appearance of a firm cake. When dressed on one side, turn it carefully, and dress it on the other. It will be dressed sufficiently when it is lightly browned. Serve it on a dish.

Egg Balls, (for made dishes or soup.)—*Time, twenty min-utes to boil the eggs.*—Pound the hard-boiled yolks of eight eggs in a mortar until very smooth; then mix with them the yolk of four raw eggs, a little salt, and a dust or so of flour to make them bind. Roll them into small balls, boil them in water, and then add them to any made dishes or soups for which they may be required.

———o———

DESERTS.

To Make Floating Islands.—Scald any tart apples before they are fully ripe, pulp them through a sieve, beat the whites of two eggs with sugar, mix it by degrees with the pulp and beat all together; serve it on raspberry cream, or color it with currant jelly, and set it on a white cream, having given it the flavor of lemon, sugar and wine, or it can be put on a custard.

Plain Bread Pudding.—Weigh three-quarters of a pound of any odd scraps of bread, either crust or crumb; cut them small, and pour on them a pint and a half of boiling water to soak them well. Let it stand until the water is cool; then press it out, and mash the bread smooth with the back of a spoon. Add to it a teaspoonful of powdered ginger, moist sugar to sweeten, three-quarters of a pound of picked and cleaned currants. Mix well, and lay in a pan well buttered; flatten it down with a spoon, lay some pieces of butter on the top, and bake in a moderate oven. Serve hot.

Hard Times Pudding.—*Time, three hours.*—Half a pint of molasses, half a pint of water, two teaspoonfuls of soda, one teaspoonful of salt; thicken with flour, sifted, to a batter, thick as cup cake; put into pudding-boiler, half full, to allow for swelling; boil steadily for three hours; eat with or without sauce.

Custard, Baked.—Boil a pint of cream with mace and cinnamon; when cold, take four eggs, leaving out two of the whites, a little rose and orange-flower water, a little white wine, nutmeg, and sugar to your taste; mix them well together, and bake them in china cups.

Lemon Custard.—Take the yolks of ten eggs, beaten, strain them, and whip them with a pint of cream; boil the juice of two lemons, sweetened, with the rind of one; when cold strain it into the cream and eggs; when it almost boils, put it into a dish, grate over it the rind of a lemon, and brown it with a salamander.

Apple Dumplings.—Pare a few good-sized baking apples, and roll out some paste, divide it into as many pieces as you have apples, cut two rounds from each, and put an apple under each piece, and put the other over, join the edges, tie them in cloths, and boil them one hour.

Apple Dumplings, Baked.—Make them as directed above; but instead of tying them in cloths, place them in a buttered dish, and bake them.

Suet Pudding.—Three-quarters of a pint of chopped suet, one pint of milk or water, one egg, beaten, one-half teaspoonful salt, and enough flour to make a stiff batter, but thin enough to pour from a spoon. Put into a bowl, cover with a cloth, and boil three hours. The same, made a little thinner, with a few raisins added, and baked in a well-greased dish is excellent.

POOR MAN'S PUDDING.—Into two quarts of boiling water, stir six heaping tablespoonfuls of meal, a little salt, and a piece of butter the size of an egg. When nearly cold, add three well-beaten eggs, and eight tablespoonfuls of sugar or molasses, and spice to taste.

ARROWROOT BLANCMANGE.—Mix two ounces of arrowroot with a large cupful of milk into a smooth, thick batter; boil one pint of milk with three laurel leaves until sufficiently flavored, then strain the milk into a jug and pour it over the arrowroot, stirring it constantly; add sugar to taste, and stir it over a clear fire until very thick; add a tablespoonful of brandy or of noyeau, and pour it into an oiled mold. Set it in a cold place, or in ice, if you have it. When firm, turn it carefully out on a dish, and garnish it with fruit or flowers.

CHEAP PLUM PUDDING.—One cup suet, one cup raisins, one cup currants and citron mixed, one egg, one cup sweet milk, half a teacup molasses, one teaspoonful soda, three and a half cups flour, a little salt. Boil three hours. Serve with hard or liquid sauce.

PLUM PUDDING.—A pint of bread crumbs; pour over them one half pint of boiling milk and let it cool thoroughly. Then add one pound stoned raisins, one-half pound currants, one tablespoonful of butter minced fine, one tablespoonful of flour, one tablespoonful of sugar, one small teaspoonful cloves, nutmeg, and cinnamon, each; five eggs, beaten light. Flour your fruit before mixing, and boil three hours. Eat with hot brandy sauce.

INDIAN PUDDING.—Scald one pound of Indian meal—that is, pour boiling water on it, stirring until stiff; have ready one pound chopped suet; stir it in, and add one pint molasses and one ounce ground ginger; bake in a greased tin in a slow oven; takes about two hours to bake.

OLD-FASHIONED BOILED INDIAN MEAL PUDDING.—To one quart of boiling milk stir in a pint and a half of Indian meal, well sifted, a teaspoonful of salt, a cup of molasses, chopped suet, if you like; tie it up tight in a cloth, not allowing room for it to swell, and boil four hours.

MINCE PIES.—Take equal weights of tender roast beef, suet, currants, raisins, and apples which have been previously pared and cored, with half their weight of soft sugar, one ounce of powdered cinnamon, an equal quantity of candied orange and lemon-peel, and citron, a little salt, and twelve sour almonds blanched and grated. Chop the meat and the suet separately;

wash and pick the currants, stone the raisins, and chop them with the peel; and having minced all the ingredients very fine, mix them together, adding a nutmeg.

APPLE PIE.—Pare and take out the cores of the apples, cutting each apple into four or eight pieces, according to their size. Lay them neatly in a baking-dish, seasoning with brown sugar, and any spice, such as pounded cloves and cinnamon, or grated lemon-peel. A little quince marmalade gives a fine flavor to the pie. Add a little water, and cover with puff paste. Bake for an hour.

RHUBARB PIE.—Take the tender stalks of the rhubarb; strip off the skin, and cut the stalks into thin slices. Line deep plates with pie crust, then put in the rhubarb, with a thick layer of sugar to each layer of rhubarb—a little grated lemon peel improves the pie. Cover the pies with a crust, press it down tight upon the edge of the plate, and prick the crust with a fork, so that the crust will not burst while baking, and let out the juices of the pie. Rhubarb pies should be baked about an hour, in a slow oven. It will not do to bake them quick. Some cooks stew the rhubarb before making it into pies, but it is not so good as when used without stewing.

COCOANUT PIE.—Cut off the brown part of the cocoanut; grate the white part, mix it with milk, and set it on the fire. Let it boil slowly eight or ten minutes. To a pound of the grated cocoanut allow a quart of milk, eight eggs, four table-spoonfuls of sifted white sugar, a glass of wine, a small cracker pounded fine, two spoonfuls of melted butter, and half a nutmeg. The eggs and sugar should be beaten together to a froth, then the wine stirred in. Put them into the milk and cocoanut, which should be first allowed to get quite cool; add the cracker and nutmeg, and turn the whole into deep pie-plates with a lining and rim of puff paste. Bake them as soon as turned into the plates.

SQUASH PIES.—Boil and sift a good, dry squash, thin it with boiling milk until it is about the consistency of thick milk porridge. To every quart of this add three eggs, two great spoonfuls of melted butter, nutmeg, (or ginger, if you prefer,) and sweeten quite sweet with sugar. Bake in a deep plate, with an undercrust.

PUMPKIN PIE.—Cut the pumpkin into as thin slices as possible, and in stewing it, the less water you use, the better; stir so that it shall not burn; when cooked and tender, stir in two pinches of salt; mash thoroughly, and then strain through a sieve; while hot add a tablespoonful of butter; for every measured quart of stewed pumpkin, add a quart of warm milk and four eggs, beating yolks and whites separately; sweeten with white sugar and cinnamon and nutmeg to taste, and a saltspoon of ground ginger. Before putting your pumpkin in your pies, it should be scalding hot,

CUSTARD PIE.—Beat six eggs, sweeten a quart of rich milk, that has been boiled and cooled; a stick of cinnamon, or a bit of lemon-peel should be boiled in it. Sprinkle in a salt-spoonful of salt, add the eggs and a grated nutmeg, stirring the whole together; line two plates with good paste, set them in the oven five minutes to harden; then pour in the custard, and bake twenty or twenty-five minutes.

LEMON MARINGUE PIE.—Boil three lemons until they are soft enough for a straw to penetrate the rind; mash them up fine with a tablespoonful of butter, one cup and a half of pow-dered sugar, and the yolks of six eggs; make a thin crust, put in the mixture and bake it; when cool, beat up the whites of the eggs with one and a half cups of powdered sugar, and spread it over the pie; brown it a nice color.

TOMATO PIE.—Take six or eight tomatoes, two lemons, one teaspoonful flour, and sugar to taste. Crust top and bottom.

———o———

SAUCES, ETC.

———

WHITE WINE SAUCE.—*Time, five minutes.*—Add to half a pint of good melted butter four spoonfuls of white wine, the grated rind of half a lemon, and the sugar pounded and sifted. Let it boil, and serve with plum, bread, or boiled batter pudding, etc.

PARSLEY SAUCE.—*Time, six or seven minutes.*—Wash the parsley thoroughly, boil it for six or seven minutes, till tender, then press the water well out of it; chop it very fine; make half or a quarter of a pint of melted butter, as required, (the less butter the less parsley, of course), mix it gradually with the hot melted butter.

APPLE SAUCE.—Pare, core, and slice some apples, put them with a little water into the saucepan to prevent them from burning, add a little lemon peel; when sufficiently done, take out the latter, bruise the apples, put in a bit of butter, and sweeten it.

BREAD SAUCE, for Roast Turkey or Game.—Peel and slice an onion, and simmer it in a pint of new milk until tender; break the bread into pieces, and put it into a small stewpan. Strain the hot milk over it, cover it close, and let it soak for an hour. Then beat it up smooth with a fork, add the pounded mace, cayenne, salt, and an ounce of butter; boil it up, and serve it in a tureen. The onion must be taken out before the milk is poured over the bread.

CRANBERRY SAUCE.—This sauce is very simply made. A quart of cranberries are washed and stewed with sufficient water to cover them; when they burst, mix with them a pound of brown sugar, and stir them.

TOMATO SAUCE.—Fresh tomatoes, take out stalk, press them all tightly down in a stewpan, cover them, put on the fire, strain off the liquor that is drawn from them, add to the tomatoes a slice of raw ham, two onions; let it stew for an hour, then rub it through a sieve. Have in another stewpan a little good brown sauce, put your tomato into it, boil all together, season with cayenne, salt, sugar, and lemon-juice.

CELERY SAUCE.—Three heads of fine white celery cut into two-inch lengths, keep them so, or shred them down as straws; boil them a few minutes, strain them off, return the celery into the stewpan, put either some brown or white stock, and boil it until tender; if too much liquor, reduce it by boiling, then add either white or brown sauce to it, season it with sugar, cayenne, pepper, and salt.

TOMATO CATSUP.—Boil half a bushel of tomatoes until soft —force them through a fine sieve, and put a quart of vinegar, one pint of salt, two ounces of cloves, two ounces of allspice, one and a half ounces of cayenne pepper, 1 tablespoonful of pepper, two heads of garlic, skinned; mix together and boil three hours, then bottle without being strained.

CLEAR GRAVY.—Slice beef thin; broil a part of it over a very clear fire, just enough to give color to the gravy, but not to dress it; put that and the raw into a very nicely tinned stewpan, with two onions, a clove or two, whole black peppers, berries of allspice, and a bunch of sweet herbs; cover it with hot water, give it one boil, and skim it well two or three times; then cover it, and simmer till quite strong.

ARROWROOT SAUCE FOR PLUM PUDDING.—*Time, fifteen minutes.*—Rub very smoothly a dessertspoonful of arrowroot in a little water, or in a glass of white wine; squeeze in the juice of half a lemon, add the pounded sugar, and pour gradually in a half pint of water. Stir it very quickly over a clear fire until it boils. Serve it with plum pudding. This sauce may be flavored with anything you prefer.

BEEF TEA.—Beef to be used for beef tea should be cut fine or chopped, and then soaked in cold water for two hours, if the time can be spared, and placed upon the fire in the same water. After thorough boiling it should be strained, all the fat carefully removed, and a little salt added. Allow a pint of water to every pound of meat.

LOBSTER SALAD.—Take one or two heads of white heart lettuce; they should be as fresh as possible; lay them in spring water for an hour or two; then carefully wash them, and trim off all the withered or cankered leaves; let them drain awhile, and dry them lightly in a clean napkin; from the lobster take out the coral or red meat, and mince the remaining parts very fine. Mash the coral fine with the yolks of four hard boiled eggs, a little sweet-oil, mustard, pepper, and salt, all mixed well, and moistened with vinegar; incorporate this mixture thoroughly with the meat; put it on a dish; sprinkle the whole with lettuce minced very fine.

A CHEAP BROWN GRAVY.—*Time, two hours.*—Take a pound of gravy beef and a sheep's melt, cut it into slices, dredge them with flour, and fry them lightly in butter; then pour in hot quite a pint of water. Add a seasoning of pepper and salt, a small onion, and a piece of celery cut into slices. Set the stew-pan over the fire, and let it stew slowly for two hours. Skim it well; strain it; add a spoonful of catsup, and set it by for use.

MUSHROOM SAUCE.—Stew one teacupful of mushrooms in just water enough to cover them; drain them, use a seive; add one teacupful of milk, three tablespoonfuls of butter, with a little nutmeg, mace, salt and pepper; stew over a good fire until it begins to thicken, then wet a teaspoonful of flour with cold milk, and stir it in until it comes to a boil. Serve in a sauce-boat, or pour over boiled chickens or rabbits.

MINT SAUCE.—Take some green mint and chop it fine; for every heaping tablespoonful of the chopped mint add one even teaspoonful of sugar and a wineglassful of cider vinegar; put the vinegar and sugar in a sauce-boat, then add the mint; let it stand fifteen minutes before serving.

———o———

PICKLES.

GREEN PICKLES FOR DAILY USE.—A gallon of vinegar, three quarters of a pound of salt, quarter pound of ginger, an ounce of mace, quarter ounce of Cayenne pepper, and an ounce of mustard seed, simmered in vinegar, and when cold put in a jar. You may throw in fresh vegetables when you choose.

TO PICKLE BEET.—Wash it, but do not cut off any of the rootlets; boil or bake it tender, peel it, or rub off the outside with a coarse cloth, cut it into slices, put it into a jar, with cold boiled vinegar, black pepper and ginger.

CHOW-CHOW.—A peck of tomatoes, two quarts of green peppers, half a peck of onions, two cabbages cut as for slaw, and two quarts of mustard seed. Have a large firkin, put in a layer of sliced tomatoes, then one of onions; next one of peppers, lastly cabbage; sprinkle over some of the mustard seed, repeat the layers again, and so on until you have used up the above quantity. Boil a gallon of vinegar with a bit of alum, two ounces of cloves and two of allspice tied in a little bag and boiled with the vinegar, skim it well and turn into the firkin. Let it stand twenty-four hours, then pour the whole into a large kettle, and let it boil five minutes; turn into the firkin, and stand away for future use.

PEPPERS.—These are done in the same manner as cucumbers. If you do not like them very fiery, first extract the seeds. Peppers should never be put in the same jar with cucumbers; but tomatoes are much improved by being pickled with them. The bell pepper is the best for pickling. It should be gathered before it shows any signs of turning red. Peppers do not require any spice. They may be stuffed like mangoes.

To PICKLE RED CABBAGE.—Cut the cabbage across in very thin slices, lay it on a large dish, sprinkle a good handful of salt over it, and cover it with another dish; let it stand twenty-four hours, put it in a colander to drain, and then lay it in the jar. Take white-wine vinegar sufficient to cover it, a little mace, cloves and allspice, and put them in whole, with one pennyworth of cochineal bruised fine, and some whole pepper. Boil it all up together, let it stand till cold, then pour it over the cabbage, and tie the jar over with leather.

To PICKLE CUCUMBERS.—Let your cucumbers be small, fresh-gathered, and free from spots; then make a pickle of salt and water, strong enough to bear up an egg; boil the pickle and skim it well, and then pour it on the cucumbers, and stir them down for twenty-four hours; strain them out in a colander, and dry them well with a cloth; take the best wine or cider vinegar, cloves, mace, nutmeg, pepper and race ginger, boil them up together, put the cucumbers in with a little salt; as soon as they begin to turn their color, put into jars, and when cold tie on a bladder or leather.

To PICKLE ONIONS.—Peel and boil them in milk and water a few moments; put cloves, spice, pepper and salt into your vinegar, boil it in brass, turn it on your onions, and cover them tight.

ONIONS.—Boil some water with salt, pour it over the onions hot, let them stand all night, then peel and put them into cold salt and water. Boil double-distilled vinegar with white spice, and when cold, put your onions in a jar and pour the vinegar over them; tie them tight down with leather. Mind always to keep pickles tied down close, or they will spoil.

———o———

BREAD, BISCUITS AND PASTRY.

FAMILY BREAD.—Take eight pounds of fine wheat flour, and sift it into your bread-dish: rub well into the flour a table-spoonful of lard or butter. Make a deep hole in the middle of the flour, and having ready a quart of water, lukewarm, with a heaped tablespoonful of fine salt, mix it with flour and yeast, pour it into the cavity; take a large spoon and stir in the surrounding flour until you have a thick batter; then scatter a handful of flour over the dish, cover up your batter and put it in a warm place, if it is cold weather; if summer anywhere will be warm enough. This is called *setting a sponge.* When the batter shows pretty determined signs of fermentation, pour in as much warm water as will make the whole mass of the flour and batter of a proper consistence. Knead it well, until it is perfectly clean and smooth; put it directly into your bread pans, which must be first well greased. In about half an hour it will be ready to put in the oven, which should be properly heated beforehand.

MILK BREAD.—*Time, one hour.*—One pint of boiling water, one pint of new milk, one teaspoonful soda, the same of salt, flour enough to form a batter: let it rise, add sufficient flour to form a dough, and bake immediately.

CORN BREAD.—*Time, one hour and a half.*—Take one quart of sweet milk, corn meal enough to thicken, three eggs, half a cup of butter, two tablespoonfuls of brown sugar, one teaspoonful of soda, and two of cream of tartar; bake in a moderate oven.

BROWN BREAD.—*Time, four or five hours.*—One quart of Indian meal and one quart of rye, mixed well together; half a cup of molasses, one tablespoonful of salt, tablespoonful of cream of tartar, two-thirds of a tablespoonful of soda, dissolved in a pint of cold water. When dissolved wet the mixture with it, and if it does not thoroughly wet it add a little more. It should be nearly as stiff as bread.

RYE AND INDIAN BREAD.—There are many different proportions of mixing it—some put one-third Indian meal with two of rye; others like one-third rye and two of Indian; others prefer it half and half.

If you use the largest proportion of rye meal, make your dough stiff, so that it will mould into loaves; when it is two-thirds Indian, it should be softer, and baked in deep earthen or tin pans, after the following rule:

Take 2 quarts of sifted Indian meal; put it into a glazed earthen pan, sprinkle over it a tablespoonful of fine salt; pour over it about a quart of boiling water, stir and work it till every part of the meal is thoroughly wet; Indian meal absorbs a greater quantity of water. When it is about milk-warm, work in 1 quart of rye meal and a teacupful of lively yeast, mixed with half a pint of warm water; add more warm water, if needed. Work the mixture well with your hands; it should be stiff, but not firm us flour dough. Have ready a large, deep, well-buttered pan; put in the dough and smooth the top by putting your hand in warm water, and then patting down the loaf. Set this to rise in a warm place in the winter; in the summer it should not be put by the fire. When it begins to crack on the top, which will usually be in about an hour or an hour and a half, put it into a well-heated oven, and bake it nearly 3 hours. It is better to let it stand in the oven all night, unless the weather is warm. Indian meal requires to be well cooked. The loaf will weigh about 4 pounds. Pan bread keeps best in large loaves.

MUFFINS.—Take 1 pint of new milk, 1 pint of hot water, 4 lumps of sugar, 1 egg, half a pint of good brisk yeast, and flour enough to make the mixture quite as thick as pound cake. Let it rise well; bake in hoops on a griddle.

EXCELLENT BISCUITS.—Take of flour 2 lbs., carbonate of ammonia 3 drachms in fine powder, white sugar 4 oz., arrowroot 1 oz., butter 4 oz., 1 egg; mix into a stiff paste with new milk, and beat them well with a rolling-pin for half an hour; roll out thin, and cut them out with a docker, and bake in a quick oven for 15 minutes.

TO MAKE FRENCH BREAD AND FRENCH ROLLS.—Mix the yolks of twelve eggs and the whites of eight. beaten and strained, a peck of fine flour and a quart of good yeast (but not bitter) with as much warm milk as will make the whole into a thin light dough; stir it well, but do not knead it. Put the dough into dishes, and set it to rise; then turn it into a quick oven; when done rasp the loaves.

French rolls are made by rubbing into every pound of flour an ounce of butter, one egg beaten, a little yeast, and sufficient milk to make a dough moderately stiff; beat it up, but do not knead it. Let it rise and bake in rolls on tins; when baked, rasp them.

INDIAN JOHNNY CAKE.—1 quart of Indian meal, 1 cup of flour, 2 eggs, 1 cup of molasses, 1 teaspoonful of saleratus, 1 of ginger, then stir in the meal.

TEA BISCUIT.—One quart of sifted flour, a little salt, three teaspoonfuls Royal baking powder, a small handful of sugar; mix lightly through the flour; rub a large teaspoonful of lard through the dry mixture; mix with sweet milk or water, the colder the better; roll out soft to thickness of about one-third of an inch; cut with a large-sized cutter, and bake in a really hot oven.

FLOUR MUFFINS.—*Time, fifteen minutes.*—One-half cup of butter, one-half cup of sugar, two cups of milk, three teaspoonfuls of yeast powder rubbed thoroughly into a scant quart of flour, and a little salt; bake in muffin rings.

CORN MUFFINS.—*Time, fifteen minutes.*—Two cups yellow
Indian meal, one cup flour, three eggs, four tablespoonfuls of
sugar, and a little salt, a piece of lard or butter the size of an
egg, one teaspoonful saleratus and two of cream tartar (the
cream tartar must be put in dry with the flour, and the saleratus mixed with a little warm water and put in last of all);
mix all together with milk as thick as pound-cake batter.
Pour in corn-muffin pans, and bake in a hot oven.

PLAIN BISCUITS.—One pound flour, half a pint of milk, two
ounces and a half of fresh butter.
Dissolve the butter in the milk made warm but not hot, and
stir it into the flour to make a firm paste; roll it out thin with
a plain tin shape or a tumbler; prick each biscuit and bake.

PASTE FOR CUSTARDS.—Rub six ounces of butter into half
a pound of flour. Mix it well together with two beaten eggs
and three tablespoonfuls of cream. Let it stand a quarter of
an hour; then work it up, and roll out very thin for use.

COMMON YEAST.—Thicken two quarts of water with fine
flour, about three spoonfuls; boil it half an hour, sweeten it
with half a spoonful of brown sugar; when nearly cold put into it four spoonfuls of fresh yeast and pour it into a jug, shake
it well together, and let it stand one day to ferment near the
fire without being covered. There will be a thin liquor on the
top, which must be poured off; shake the remainder and cork
it up for use. Take always four spoonfuls of the old mixture to ferment the next quantity, keeping it always in succes-
ion: A half-peck loaf will require about a gill.

————o————

CAKES, TARTS, ETC., ETC.

PLUM CAKE OR WEDDING CAKE.—One pound of dry flour,
one pound of sweet butter, one pound of sugar, twelve eggs,
two pounds of raisins, (the sultana raisins are the best), two
pounds of currants. As much spice as you please. A glass of
wine, one of brandy, and a pound of citron. Mix the butter
and sugar as for pound-cake. Sift the spice, and beat the eggs
very light. Put in the fruit last, stirring it in gradually. It
should be well floured. If necessary, add more flour after the
fruit is in. Butter sheets of paper and line the inside of one
large pan, or two smaller ones. Lay in some slices of citron,
then a layer of the mixture, then of the citron, and so on till
the pan is full. This cake requires a tolerably hot and steady
oven, and will need baking 4 or 5 hours, according to its thick-

ness. It will be better to let it cool gradually in the oven. Ice it when thoroughly cold.

MARBLE CAKE.—*White Part.*—Whites of four eggs, one cup white sugar, half cup of butter, half cup of sweet milk, two teaspoonfuls of baking-powder, one teaspoonful of vanilla or lemons, and two and a half cups of sifted flour. *Black part.*—

Yolks of four eggs, one cup brown sugar, half cup molasses, half cup butter, half cup sour milk, one teaspoonful cloves, one teaspoonful cinnamon, one teaspoonful mace, one nutmeg, one teaspoonful soda, and one and a half cups sifted flour. Put it in the cake-dish alternately, first one part and then the other. The tin should be lined with buttered paper.

MACAROONS.—Pound well in a mortar with the white of an egg half a pound of sweet almonds blanched, with a few bitter ones also blanched. Beat to a froth the whites of four eggs, and mix with them 2 lbs. of sugar. Mix all together, and drop them on paper placed on a tin. A half an hour in a gentle oven bakes them.

SPONGE CAKE.—Five eggs, half a pound of sugar, and a quarter of a pound of flour.

ANOTHER.—One pound of sugar, nine eggs, the weight of four eggs of flour; beat the yolks and white separate; mix the sugar and eggs together before you add the flour; a little nutmeg.

CHOCOLATE CAKE.—Two cups of sugar, one half cup of butter, whites of three eggs, one cup of milk, two and three-fourths cups of flour, three teaspoonfuls of baking powder; bake on jelly-tins; whites of two eggs, well beaten, with not quite a cup of pulverized sugar; add six tablespoonfuls of grated German sweet chocolate, and two teaspoonfuls of vanilla; spread the cakes.

LEMON CAKE.—One cup butter, three cups sugar, four cups flour, one cup milk, five eggs, one teaspoonful soda, juice and rind of one lemon.

LOAF CAKE.—Five pounds of flour, two of sugar, one and a half of butter, eight eggs, one quart of milk; roll the sugar with the flour, add yeast sufficient to make it rise, and then add the raisins and spice.

GINGER CAKE.—Two and a half pounds flour, 1 of butter, 1 of sugar, four eggs, one pint of molasses, teaspoonful and a half of pearlash, one half pint of milk, two ounces of ginger, two pounds of currants, half a pound of raisins and a few cloves.

WASHINGTON CAKE.—Beat six eggs very light, add one pound of butter, one of sugar, and one pint of rich milk a little sour, a glass of wine, a ground nutmeg, a spoonful of saleratus; bake in tins or small pans in a brisk oven.

JUMBLES.—Stir together, till of a light color, a pound of sugar and half the weight of butter—then add eight eggs, beaten to a froth, essence of lemon, or rose-water, to the taste, and flour to make them sufficiently stiff to roll out. Roll them out in powdered sugar, about half an inch thick, cut it into strips about half an inch wide, and four inches long, join the ends together, so as to form rings, lay them on flat tins that have been buttered, and bake them in a quick oven.

JELLY CAKE.—Beat three eggs well, the whites and yolks separately; take a cup of fine white sugar and beat that in well with the yolks, and a cupful of sifted flour stirred in gently; then stir in the whites, a little at a time, a teaspoonful of baking powder and one tablespoonful of milk, pour it in three jelly cake plates, and bake from five to ten minutes in a well heated oven, and when cold spread with currant jelly, and place each layer on top of the other and sift powdered sugar on the top.

SEED CAKE.—Mix quarter of peck of flour with half pound of sugar, quarter of an ounce of allspice, and a little ginger; melt three-quarters of a pound of butter with half pint of milk; when just warm, put to it quarter of a pint of yeast, and work up to a good dough. Let it stand before the fire a few minutes before it goes to the oven; add seeds or currants; bake one hour and a half.

A PLAIN CAKE.—Mix together three-quarters of a pound of flour, the same of moist sugar, a quarter of a pound of butter, one egg, well beaten, and two tablespoonfuls of milk; bake moderately.

CRANBERRY TART.—Pick a quart of cranberries free from all imperfections, put a pint of water to them, and put them into a stewpan; add a pound of fine brown sugar to them, and set them over the fire to stew gently until they are soft; then mash them with a silver spoon, and turn them into a pie-dish to become cold. Put a puff-paste around the edge of the dish, and cover it over with a crust, or make an open tart in a flat dish with paste all over the bottom of it, and around the edge; put in the cranberries; lay cross-bars of paste over the top, and bake.

OPEN TARTS.—These are tarts without covers, made in flat dishes. Cover the bottom of the dish with a common paste; then cut a strip of puff-paste and lay around the edge of the dish. Fill in the center with any jam or preserved fruit. Decorate the top of the jam with narrow bars of paste, crossed all over, or stamped leaves. Bake for half an hour.

CHERRY TART.—Take about one pound and a half of cherries, half a pound of short crust, and moist sugar to taste.

Pick the stalks from the cherries, put a tiny cup upside down in the middle of a deep pie-dish, fill around it with the fruit, and add moist sugar to taste. Lay some short crust around the edge of the dish, put on the cover as directed before, ornament the edges, and bake it in a quick oven. When ready to serve, sift some loaf sugar over the top.

RHUBARB TART.—Cut the large stalks from the leaves, strip off the outside skin and cut the sticks into pieces half an inch long. Line a pie dish with paste rolled rather thicker than a dollar piece, put in a layer of rhubarb, strew the sugar over it, then fill it up with the other pieces of stalks, cover it with a rich puff paste, cut a slit in the center, trim off the edge with a knife and bake it in a quick oven. Glaze the top or strew sugar over it.

PLAIN APPLE TART.—Rub a pie-dish over with butter, line it with short pie crust rolled thin, pare some cooking apples, cut them in small pieces, fill the pie-dish with them, strew over them a cupful of fine moist sugar, three or four cloves or a little grated lemon peel, and add a few spoonfuls of water; then cover with puff-paste crust, trim off the edges with a sharp knife and cut a small slit at each end, pass a gigling iron around the pie half an inch inside the edge, and bake in a quick oven.

CRULLERS.—One cup of sugar, one cup of buttermilk or sour milk, three tablespoonfuls of melted butter, one egg, one teaspoonful of saleratus; flavor with nutmeg, a little salt; mix as soft as possible, and cut any desired shape. Have your fat hot. If a piece of raw potato be peeled and thrown in the fat, it will keep the crullers from burning.

DOUGHNUTS.—Half a pint of sweet milk, half a cup of butter, (scant), one cup of yeast, salt; flavor with nutmeg or cinnamon. Mix them at night. In the morning roll out and let them raise until very light, and drop in hot fat. They are very nice, after they are fried, to roll them in pulverized sugar.

GINGER SNAPS.—Take two tea-cups of molasses, one of butter, and one of sugar. Boil the butter and sugar together. Add a tablespoonful of black pepper, two of ginger, a teaspoonful of saleratus, and flour to roll out. Roll them thin; cut in shapes and bake quick. These are very nice, and the longer they are kept the better they will be.

COOKIES.—To three cups of sugar put one of butter, one of milk, three eggs, a teaspoonful of saleratus dissolved in the milk, and carraway seeds, if you like, or other spice.

FROSTING FOR CAKE.—For the white of one egg, 9 heaping teaspoons of white refined sugar, 1 Poland starch. Beat the eggs to a stiff froth so that you can turn the plate upside down without the eggs falling off, stir in the sugar slowly with a wooden spoon, 10 or 15 minutes constantly; to frost a common-sized cake 1 egg and a half.

A Charlotte Russe.—Cut as many very thin slices of white bread as will cover the bottom and line the sides of a baking-dish, but first rub it thick with butter. Put apples, in thin slices, into the dish, in layers, till full, strewing sugar between and bits of butter. In the meantime, soak as many slices of bread as will cover the whole, in warm milk, over which lay a plate and a weight to keep the bread close on the apples. Bake slowly three hours. To a middling-sized dish use half a pound of butter in the whole.

Molasses Gingerbread.—One egg, one tablespoon butter, two-thirds cup molasses, half cup milk, one teaspoon soda, two and one half cups flour, one tablespoon ginger, one teaspoon cream tartar, salt; sour milk may be used, but if so, use one cup, two teaspoons soda and no cream tartar.

———o———

GRIDDLE CAKES, PAN CAKES, ETC.. ETC., ETC.

———

Buckwheat Cakes.—Let the buckwheat be of the hulled sort, and fresh. Put into a two-quart pitcher one and a half pints of tepid water; add four tablespoonfuls of bakers' or as much "compressed" yeast as will make one loaf of bread—other kinds in proportion—with a little salt. Then stir in buckwheat enough to make a thick batter; cover the pitcher and set away to rise over night, after beating thoroughly. In the morning add three tablespoonfuls of molasses and a quarter of a teaspoonful of soda, dissolved in about three tablespoonfuls of milk. Beat all well together, and pour the cakes from the pitcher upon a well-heated griddle.

Graham Griddle Cakes.—*Time, five minutes.*—One pint of milk, half a cup of sour cream, half a teaspoonful of soda, the same of salt; stir in Graham flour not as stiff as for fine flour cakes, (no eggs); have the griddle quite hot; or with yeast the same as with buckwheat.

Rice Cakes.—Boil a cupful of rice until it becomes a jelly; while it is warm, mix a large lump of butter with it and a little salt. Add as much milk to a small teacupful of flour as will make a tolerable stiff batter—stir it until it is quite smooth, and then mix it with the rice. Beat six eggs as light as possible, and add them to the rice.
These cakes are fried on a griddle as all other pancakes—they must be carefully turned.

Serve them with powdered sugar and nutmeg. They should be served as hot as possible, or they will become heavy—and a heavy pancake is a very poor affair.

WAFFLES.—Take a quart of flour, and wet it with a little sweet milk; then stir in enough milk to form a thick batter. Add a tablespoonful of melted butter, two eggs well-beaten, a teaspoonful of salt, and yeast to raise it. When light, heat your waffle iron, by placing it on a bed of clear, bright coals; grease it well, and fill it with the batter. Two or three minutes will suffice to bake on one side; then turn the iron over; and when brown on both sides, the cake is done. Butter the waffles as soon as done, and serve with powdered white sugar and cinnamon; or you may put on the sugar and spice at the same time with the butter.

INDIAN GRIDDLE CAKES.—1 quart of milk, 6 eggs, teaspoonful of saleratus, some nutmeg, teaspoonful of salt, stir meal in until you have a thick batter, fry in melted butter and lard.

APPLE FRITTERS.—Beat and strain the yolks of seven eggs, and the whites of three; mix into them a pint of new milk, a little grated nutmeg, a pinch of salt, and a glass of brandy. Well beat the mixture, and then add gradually sufficient flour to make a thick batter. Pare and core six large apples, cut them in slices about a quarter of an inch thick, sprinkle pounded sugar over them, and set them by for an hour or more; dip each piece of apple in the batter, and fry them in hot lard about six minutes; the lard should not be made too hot at first, but must become hotter as they are frying. Serve on a napkin with sifted sugar over them.

SNOW PANCAKES.—Make a stiff batter with four ounces of flour, a quarter of a pint of milk, or more if required, a little grated nutmeg, and a pinch of salt. Divide the batter into any number of pancakes, and add three large spoonfuls of snow to each. Fry them lightly, in very good butter, and serve quickly.

————o————

PRESERVES, JELLIES, JAMS, ETC.

———

STRAWBERRY JAM.—To six pounds of strawberries allow three pounds of sugar. Procure some fine scarlet strawberries, strip off the stalks, and put them into a preserving pan over a moderate fire; boil them for half an hour, keeping them constantly stirred. Break the sugar into small pieces and mix it with the strawberries after they have been removed from the fire. Then place it again over the fire, and boil it for another half hour very quickly. Put it into pots, and when cold cover it over with brandy papers and a piece of paper moistened with the white of an egg over the tops.

APPLE MARMALADE.—Take a peck of apples, full grown, but not the least ripe, of all or any sort; quarter them and take out the cores, but do not pare them; put them into a preserving pan with one gallon of water, and let them boil moderately until you think the pulp will run, or suffer itself to be squeezed through a cheese-cloth, only leaving the peels behind. Then to each quart of pulp add one pound, good weight, of loaf sugar, either broken in small pieces or pounded, and boil it all together for half an hour and ten minutes, keeping it stirred; then put it into pots, the larger the better, as it keeps longer in a large body.

GOOSEBERRY JAM.—Three pounds of loaf sugar, six pounds of rough red gooseberries. Pick off the stalks and buds from the gooseberries, and boil them carefully but quickly for rather more than half an hour, stirring continually; then add the sugar, pounded fine, and boil the jam quickly for half an hour, stirring it all the time to prevent its sticking to the preserving pan. When done put it into pots, cover it with brandy paper, and secure it closely down with paper moistened with the white of an egg.

PINE-APPLES.—Take pine-apples as ripe as you can possibly get them, pare them, and cut them into thin slices. Weigh them, and to each pound of pine-apple allow a pound of loaf-sugar. Place a layer of the pine-apple slices in the bottom of a large, deep dish, and sprinkle it thickly with a layer of the sugar, which must first be powdered. Then put another layer of the pine-apple, and sugar it well; and so on till the dish is full, finishing with a layer of sugar on the top. Cover the dish, and let it stand all night. In the morning remove the slices of pine-apple to a tureen. Pour the syrup into a preserving kettle, and skim it at least half an hour. Do not remove it from the fire, till the scum has entirely ceased to rise. Then pour the syrup, boiling hot, over the slices of pine-apple in the tureen. Cover it and let it stand till cold. Then transfer the sliced pine-apple and the syrup to wide-mouthed glass jars, or cover them well, pasting down thick white paper over the top.

ᶠ ORANGE MARMALADE.—Take six pounds of oranges; cut the peel so as to make it peel off in four pieces. Put all the peels on the fire in a preserving-pan, with a large quantity of water, and boil them for two hours, then cut them in very thin slices. While they are boiling, press the inside of the oranges through a splinter sieve, narrow enough to prevent the seeds and skin from going through. When this is done, and the peels cut into the thinnest shreds, put the whole on a fire in a copper or brass pan, with eight pounds of loaf sugar broken small, Boil it all together for ten minutes; it may then be taken off the fire and put into preserving jars.

GRAPE JELLY.—Take grapes before they are fully ripe, and boil them gently with a very little water; then strain and proceed as with currant jelly. Wild grapes will not make as firm a jelly as cultivated ones.

• WINE JELLY.—To one and a half boxes gelatine, one pint cold water, juice of three lemons, grated rind of two; let stand an hour, then add two pounds of loaf sugar, three pints boiling water; boil five minutes; just before straining in flannel bag, stir in one pint sherry wine, six tablespoonfuls of best brandy.

GOOSEBERRY JAM.—To every pound of gooseberries add a pound of sugar; bruise the gooseberries in a mortar, and boil them well. When cold put the jam in pots.

PRESERVED STRAWBERRIES.—Pick off all the stems, and to every quart of fruit add a quart of sugar; mix well with the sugar, and put them over a slow fire till the syrup commences to form, then put them over a hot fire, and let them boil quickly for fifteen minutes, skimming it well. Put them boiling hot into stone jars, seal up tightly.

CALVES' FOOT JELLY.—For one mould, chop up two calves' feet, put them on in about four quarts of water to boil—this should be done the day before you require the jelly—keep it well skimmed and boil gently all day; it will then be reduced to about two quarts; the next morning take off all the grease, and wash the top with a little warm water, then rinse it with cold, place the stock in the proper size stewpan to allow it to boil well; then put in a paring of lemon, without any white adhering to it, two or three cloves, a piece of cinnamon, a few bruised coriander seeds, and a bay leaf; let it boil a few minutes, then take it off to get cool. Have ready, broken in a basin, six or eight whites of eggs and the shells, chop them up together, squeeze five or six lemons, strain the juice, add sugar to the whites of eggs and a glass of cold water, then add the lemon juice; add all this well mixed into the calves' foot stock, place it on your fire, and let it rise to the top of your stewpan; be careful it does not go over; then take it off the fire, place it on the cover, and put some hot coals upon it; let it stand a few minutes, then run it repeatedly through the jelly-bag until beautifully bright and clear; flavor it with what may be required.

APPLE JAM.—Core and pare a good quantity of apples, chop them well, allow equal weight of apples and sugar; make a syrup of your sugar by adding a little water, boiling and skimming well, then throw in some grated lemon peel and a little white ginger with the apples; boil until the fruit looks clear.

GREEN GAGE JAM.—Rub ripe green gages through a sieve, put all the pulp into a pan with an equal weight of loaf sugar pounded and sifted. Boil the whole till sufficiently thick, and put into pots.

ⴼ PRESERVED LEMON PEEL.—Make a thick syrup of white sugar, chop the lemon peel fine and boil it in the syrup ten minutes; put in glass tumblers and paste paper over. A teaspoonful of this makes a loaf of cake, or a dish of sauce nice.

RASPBERRY JELLY.—This is the most agreeable of all jellies. Crush the raspberries, and strain them through a wet cloth. Put the juice into a preserving-pan, with three-quarters of a pound of sugar to one pound of juice; boil it ten minutes, and take care that it does not darken; remove the pan from the fire: strain the juice through a bag and pour it into pots. Do not touch the bag till all the jelly has passed through, else it may become thick.

BRANDY PEACHES, PLUMS, ETC.—Gather peaches before they are quite ripe, prick them with a large needle, and rub off the down with a piece of flannel. Cut a quill and pass it carefully around the stone to loosen it. Put them into a large preserving-pan, with cold water rather more than enough to cover them, and let the water become gradually scalding hot. If the water does more than simmer very gently, or if the fire be fierce, the fruit will be likely to crack. When they are tender, lift them carefully out, and fold them up in flannel or a soft tablecloth, in several folds. Have ready a quart, or more, as the peaches require, of the best white brandy, and dissolve ten ounces of powdered sugar in it. When the peaches are cool, put them into a glass jar, and pour the brandy and sugar over them. Cover with leather and a bladder. Apricots and plums in the same way.

————o————

COFFEE, TEA AND CHOCOLATE.

———

EXCELLENT COFFEE.—*For three Breakfast cups.*—Take four tablespoonfuls of roasted coffee berries, and put them in the oven till well warmed through; then grind them. Put the coffee in the pot, which should have a piece of tin over the middle strainer to prevent the coffee from filling up the holes; pour in three teacupfuls of boiling water. The breakfast cup should be filled with boiling milk.

Of tea little need be said; almost every one knows the rules for making it.

Boiling water should alone be used.

Metal teapots in preference to earthenware.

Silver is better than either,

A spoonful ot tea for each person. Heat the teapot first with some boiling water, then pour that into the teacups to warm them; put in your tea, and pour enough water on to the tea to cover it; let it stand three or four minutes, then nearly fill the teapot with water, let it stand a few minutes, and pour out, leaving some portion of tea in the pot when you replenish, that all the strength may not be poured away in the first cup.

CHOCOLATE.—*Time, ten to twelve minutes.*—Scrape up about a quarter of a pound of the chocolate cake into a saucepan with two gills of water; set it on the fire; stir it constantly with a wooden spoon until it is rather thick, then work it very quickly with the spoon. Stir in a pint of boiling milk by degrees and serve it.

SUBSTITUTE FOR CREAM IN COFFEE OR TEA.—The white of an egg beaten to a froth, mixed with a lump of butter as big as a hazel-nut. Pour on the coffee gradually, so it will not curdle, and you can hardly distinguish the preparation from fresh cream.

———o———

USEFUL RECIPES.

———

COLD IN THE HEAD.—This can be cured at once if taken in time. Dissolve a tablespoonful of pulverized borax in a pint of hot water; when tepid, snuff some up the nostrils two or three times a day; or use the dry powdered borax like snuff, taking a pinch as often as required.

HOARSENESS OR TICKLING IN THE THROAT.—Take a small quantity of dry pulverized borax, place it on the tongue, and let it slowly dissolve, and run down the throat. It is also good to keep the throat moist at night, and prevent coughing.

TO CURE FRECKLES.—Mix together two ounces of lemon juice, one drachm of pulverized borax, one half drachm of sugar; allow them to stand in a bottle for a few days. Rub occasionally over the face and hands.

TO REMOVE STAINS FROM THE HANDS.—A few drops of oil vitriol (sulphuric acid) in water, will take the stains of fruit, dark dyes, stove blacking, etc., from the hands without injuring them. Care must, however, be taken not to drop it upon the clothes. It will remove the color from woolen, and eat holes in cotton fabrics

To Remove Rust.—To remove rust from steel, cover with sweet oil well rubbed on; in forty eight hours use unslacked lime powdered very fine. Rub it till the rust disappears. To prevent rust, mix with fat oil varnish four-fifths of well-rectified spirits of turpentine. Apply the varnish by means of a sponge. Articles varnished in this manner will retain their brilliancy, and never contract any spots of rust. It may be applied to copper philosophical instruments, etc.

To Prepare an Invigorating Bath.—A tablespoonful or more of pulverized borax thrown into the bath-tub while bathing, will communicate a velvety softness to the water, and at the same time invigorate the bather. Persons troubled with nervousness or wakeful nights, will find this kind of bath very beneficial—more so than sea-bathing.

To Clean Silver.—Table silver should be cleaned at least once or twice a week, and can easily be kept in good order, and polished brightly. Have your dish-pan half full of boiling water; place the silver in so that it may become warm, then, with a soft cloth dipped into the hot water, soaped and sprinkled with pulverized borax, scour well; rinse in clear hot water; dry with a clean, dry cloth.

Spruce Beer.—Take four ounces of hops, boil half an hour in one gallon of water, strain it, add sixteen gallons of warm water, two gallons of molasses, eight ounces of essence of spruce dissolved in one quart of water; put it in a clean cask, shake it well together, add a half pint of yeast, let it stand and work one week; if warm weather, less time will do. When drawn off, add one spoonful of molasses to each bottle.

Cottage Beer.—Take a peck of good wheat bran, and put it into ten gallons of water, with three handfuls of good hops, and boil the whole together until the bran and hops sink to the bottom. Then strain it through a hair sieve, or a thin cloth, into a cooler, and when it is about lukewarm add two quarts of molasses. As soon as the molasses is melted, pour the whole into a ten-gallon cask, with two tablespoonfuls of yeast. When the fermentation has subsided, bung up the cask, and in four days it will be ready to use.

To Brighten a Copper Boiler.—Use a coarse cloth, have a pail of very hot water, soap the cloth a little, sprinkle on plenty of pulverized borax, and rub the boiler well; rinse off with hot water, and dry with a soft cloth. This is much better and safer than using acid.

Cage Birds.—Reared birds are exposed to several maladies, partly because their first nourishment consists of unnatural food, and partly, also, because pet birds have all kinds of delicacies given to them. They therefore rarely attain to the age of six years. They remain most healthy and live longest, when they have neither sugar, pastry, nor other delicacies given them, but are fed constantly on rape-seed, intermixed occasionally, by way of treat, with hemp, and occasionally a little green food, which cleanses their stomachs. They are more healthy, also, if they have some water and sand placed in the cage, that they may pick up grains to assist in the process of digestion. The remedy for moulting is a rusty nail placed in the drinking vessel, good food and ants' eggs, if accustomed to the latter when young.

———o———

MISCELLANEOUS.

TOASTED CHEESE.—Cut equal quantities of cheese, and having pared it into *extremely* small pieces, place it in a pan with a little milk, and a small slice of butter. Stir it over a slow fire until melted and quite smooth. Take it off the fire quickly, mix the yolk of an egg with it, and brown it in a toaster before the fire.

OATMEAL PORRIDGE.—*Time, half an hour.*—Put a pint of warm water into a stewpan over the fire, and as it boils dredge in two ounces of oatmeal with your left hand, and stir with the right. When it is made, turn it into a soup-plate, adding a little salt, or a little sugar, according to taste. Send it to table with a jug of hot milk, which should be added to it by degrees for eating.

TO COOK HOMINY.—Take three cups of water to one cup of hominy; boil slowly for three-quarters of an hour; the longer it boils the better it is; then add half a teacupful of sweet milk to one cup of hominy, then boil ten minutes more; stir it frequently while boiling.

RAGOUT OF DUCKS.—Put the gizzards, livers, necks, etc., into a pint of good, strong beef broth, or other well-seasoned stock. Season the ducks inside with salt and mixed spices. Brown them on all sides in a frying-pan, and then stew them till tender in strained stock. When nearly ready, thicken the sauce with browned flour and butter.

TO POT LOBSTERS.—Take from a hen lobster the spawn, coral, flesh, and pickings of the head and claws; pound well, and season with Cayenne, white pepper and mace, according to taste. Mix it to a firm paste with good melted butter. Pound and season the flesh from the tail, and put it into a pot, and then fill with the other paste. Cover the top of each pot with clarified butter, and keep it in a cool place.

OYSTER FORCEMEAT.—Take off the beards from half a pint of oysters, wash them well in their own liquor, and mince them very fine; mix with them the peel of half a lemon chopped small, a sprig of parsley, a seasoning of salt, nutmeg, and a *very* little Cayenne, and about an ounce of butter in small pieces. Stir into these ingredients five ounces of bread-crumbs, and when thoroughly mixed together, bind it with the yolk of an egg and part of the oyster liquor.

EGG PLANT AU GRATIN.—Peel and cut them in slices, length-wise, and arrange them in layers on a well-buttered tin, pre-viously rubbed with garlic. Put between the layers a sprink-ling of fine bread-crumbs, chopped parsley, sweet herbs, and pepper and salt to taste; pour over them some liquified butter; add a sprinkling of grated cheese and a few baked bread-crumbs; bake in the oven, and brown with a salamander.

FOWL BROILED.—Separate the back of the fowl and lay the two sides open; skewer the wings, as for roasting, season well with pepper and salt, and broil; send to table with the inside of the fowl to the surface of the dish; it is an admirable break-fast dish when a journey is to be performed.

CHICKEN CURRIE.—Cut up the chicken raw, slice onions, and fry both in butter with great care, of a fine light brown; or, if you use chickens that have been dressed, fry only the onions. Lay the joints, cut into two or three pieces each, into a stewpan, with a veal or mutton gravy, and a clove or two of garlic. Simmer till the chicken is quite tender. Half an hour before you serve it, rub smooth a spoonful or two of currie-powder, a spoonful of flour, and an ounce of butter; and add this, with four large spoonfuls of cream, to the stew. Salt to your taste. *When serving*, squeeze in a little lemon.

FRESH COD, BOILED.—The thickness of this fish being very unequal, the head and shoulders greatly preponderating, it is seldom boiled whole, because in a large fish the tail, from its thinness in comparison to the upper part of the fish, would be very much overdone. Whenever it is boiled whole, a small fish should be selected. Tie up the head and shoulders well, place it in the kettle with enough cold water to completely cover it; cast in a handful of salt. The fish, if a small one, will be cook-ed in twenty minutes after it has boiled—if large, it will take half an hour. When enough, drain it clear of the scum, and remove the string; send it to table garnished with the liver, the smelt, and the roe of the fish, scraped horse-radish, lemon sliced, and sprigs of parsley.

The tail, when separated from the body of the fish, may be cooked in a variety of fashions. Some salt rubbed into it, and hanging it two days, will render it exceedingly good when cooked. It may be spread open, and thoroughly salted, or it may be cut into fillets, and fried.

If the cod is cooked when very fresh, some salt should be rubbed down the back and the bone before boiling—it much improves the flavor, or, if hung for a day, the eyes of the fish should be removed, and salt filled in the vacancies. It will be found to give firmness to the fish, and add to the richness of the flavor.

STEWED SWEETBREADS.—After they are parboiled and cold, lard them with fat pork; put them in a stewpan, with some good veal gravy, and juice of a small lemon; stew them till very tender, and just before serving thicken with flour and butter; serve them with the gravy.

RICE CROQUETTES.—One teacupful of rice; boil in a pint of milk, and a pint of water; when boiled and hot, add a piece of butter the size of an egg, two tablespoonfuls of sugar, two eggs, juice and grated peel of one lemon; stir this up well; have ready the yolks of two eggs, beaten on a plate, cracker crumbs on another; make the rice in rolls, and dip in the egg and crumbs; fry them in butter; serve hot.

SUET PUDDING.—Mix one pound of flour very dry with half a pound of finely chopped suet, add eggs and a pinch of salt; make it into a paste with the water, beating it all rapidly together with a wooden spoon. Flour a pudding cloth, put the paste into it, tie the cloth tightly, and plunge it into boiling water. The shape may be either a roll, or a round ball. When it is done, untie the cloth, turn the pudding out, and serve very hot.

GOOSEBERRY FOOL.—Put two quarts of gooseberries in a stewpan with a quart of water; when they begin to turn yellow and swell drain the water from them and press them with the back of a spoon through a colander; sweeten them to your taste, and set them to cool. Put two quarts of milk over the fire beaten up with the yolks of four eggs and a little grated nutmeg; stir it over the fire until it begins to simmer, then take it off and stir it gradually into the cold gooseberries; let it stand until cold and serve it. The eggs may be left out and milk only may be used. Half this quantity makes a good dishful.

OMELET SOUFFLE.—Separate the whites from the yolks of
twelve eggs. Put the whites into a basin and beat them extremely fast till they form a very thick snow. Then beat six
yolks separately, with two ounces of sugar, and a dessertspoonful of orange-flower water, or just enough to flavor it to your
taste.

Before beating the eggs have ready a round tin, well greased
all over the inside with fresh butter.

When you have finished beating the six yolks mix them
very quickly with the whites, lest the snow should turn—that
is, melt into water. Put it then into the buttered tin, and
pace it in the oven. It will be so thick, if it is well and skil-
fully mixed, that there will be no fear of its running over.
Watch it well, glancing at it from time to time through a
little opening of the oven door, to see how it is going on; as
soon as it has risen very high, and is of a golden color, take it
out of the oven.

Do not suffer the omelet souffle to remain long in the oven.
If it is not watched it will fall in and become a mere *galette.*
Let the oven be of a very gentle heat, or the bottom of the
omelet will be burnt before the top is done.

Before putting the tin in the oven, you may powder the
snow with fine sugar; it crystalizes and has a very pretty
effect. As soon as the omelet is done it must be sent to table.

PUMPKIN PUDDING.—*Time, two hours.*—Pare the pumpkin
and put it down to stew, strain it through a colander; two
pounds of pumpkin to one pound of butter, one pound of sugar,
and eight eggs; beat to a froth; one wine-glass of brandy, half
wine-glass of rose water, one teaspoonful mace, cinnamon, and
nutmeg all together.

OYSTER PATTIES.—Cover some small tins, called patty-
pans, with puff paste, cut it round, and put in the center a
small piece of bread, (to prevent the top and bottom from col-
lapsing); cover it with paste, slightly pinch the edges together,
and bake in a brisk oven a quarter of an hour. Then, having
bearded and parboiled a dozen large oysters, cut them in
quarters and put them in a stew pan with an ounce of butter,
a teaspoonful of flour, mixed with their liquor, and the broth
from the beards, (which you must stew in a small saucepan,
with a little stock gravy and two or three shreds of lemon).

Season with a very little salt, a quarter of a teaspoonful of powdered mace, and the same quantity of Cayenne; then gradually add three tablespoonfuls of cream. Mix well; then, with a thin knife, open the patties, take out the bread, put in a spoonful of the oysters and cream gravy; put the covers on again and serve.

POTTED HALIBUT.—Take two pounds of halibut; cut into square pieces; salt with a teaspoonful of salt; sprinkle over the pieces a teaspoonful of pepper, and put in a dozen whole cloves, one whole Jamaica pepper, and a few shreds of mace; pour over it one-half teacupful of vinegar, a teacupful of ale or lager beer, a teaspoonful of tarragon vinegar, and lastly, an ounce of butter; put in a baking dish, have a plate on top of the fish, and bake slowly for 40 minutes.

STEWED ROCK-FISH.—Take a large rock-fish, and cut it in slices nearly an inch thick. Sprinkle it *very slightly* with salt, and let it remain for half an hour. Slice very thin a dozen large onions; put them into a stew-pan with a quarter of a pound of fresh butter, cut into bits. Set them over a slow fire, and stir them continually till they are quite soft, taking care not to let them become brown. Black-fish and bass are equally good cooked this way.

SALT COD—BOILED.--Put the fish to soak over night, in warm water; set in a warm place. The next morning take it out of the water; scrape and scrub it well with a hard brush; put it in a kettle of fresh cold water; bring it to the boiling point, and keep it at that heat until half an hour before dinner. Give it a good boil up; drain it well, and send to table with egg-sauce, or melted butter thickened with hard-boiled eggs minced fine. Many people like salt pork cut in small square pieces, and fried brown, as a sauce for salt fish. It is sometimes also minced with potato, and warmed over when first sent to table.

To STEAM A HAM.—If the ham has been hung for some time, put it into cold water, and let it soak all night, or let it lie on a damp stone sprinkled with water for two days to mellow. Wash it well, put it into a steamer—there are proper ones made for the purpose—over a pot of boiling water. Steam it for as long a time as the weight requires,

This is by far the best way of cooking a ham. It prevents waste and retains the flavor. When it is done, skin it and strew bread-raspings over it as usual. If you preserve the skin as whole as possible and cover the ham when cold with it, it will prevent its becoming dry.

PIGEON SOUP.—Take eight good pigeons; cut up two, and put them on with as much water as will make a large tureen of soup, adding the pinions, necks, gizzards and livers of the others; boil well and strain; season the whole pigeons within with mixed spices and salt, and truss them with their legs into their belly. Take a large handful of parsley, young onions, and spinach; pick and wash them clean, and shred small; then take a handful of grated bread, put a lump of butter about the size of a hen's egg in a frying-pan, and when it boils, throw in the bread, stirring well until it becomes a fine brown color.

TO STEW COLD VENISON.—Cut the meat in small slices, and put the trimmings and bones into a saucepan, with barely enough water to cover them. Let them stew two hours. Strain the liquor in a stew-pan: add to it some bits of butter rolled in flour, and whatever gravy was left of the venison. Stir in some currant jelly, and let it boil half an hour. Then put in the meat, and keep it over the fire long enough to heat it through, but do not let it boil.

CURRANT PUDDING.—An excellent family pudding may be made of the following ingredients: A pound of minced suet, a pound of bread crumbs or flour, three quarters of a pound of currants, washed and picked, a little powdered cinnamon and grated nutmeg, and a very little salt. Beat two eggs, and add as much milk to them as will wet the whole. Mix all together, tie in a cloth as previously directed, and boil for three hours.

ELDERBERRY WINE.—Take one quart of pure elderbery juice, two quarts water, three pounds sugar, (the best sugar for this purpose is what we call molasses sugar, viz.: sugar that settles from molasses into the bottom of hogsheads; mix all together, and let it ferment until it works itself clear; strain and bottle; leave the bottles uncorked until it is done working, then cork and put away in a cellar, and in a few months you will have good wine, but age will improve it.

ELDERBERRY WINE.—Boil three gallons of elderberries in two and one-half gallons of water for 20 minutes, then strain through a fine sieve, not bruising the berries; then measure the liquid into a boiler, and to every quart add one pound of moist sugar and the peel of four lemons; place on fire and heat scalding hot; add the whites of four eggs, well beaten, stirring into the liquid. When the liquor is cool place it in a keg; place a piece of toasted bread, spread with compressed yeast as you would butter, in the keg; bung the keg air-tight; a quarter of a pound of bruised ginger placed in the keg gives the wine a fine flavor; let it remain in the keg from six to eight weeks, when it will be ready to bottle.

CHOCOLATE CARAMELS.—Take of grated chocolate, milk, molasses, and sugar, each one cupful, and a piece of butter the size of an egg; boil until it will harden when dropped into cold water; add vanilla; put in a buttered pan, and before it cools mark off in square blocks.

MUSHROOM CATSUP.—Take a stewpan full of large-flap mushrooms that are not worm-eaten, the skins and fringe of those you have pickled, throw a handful of salt among them, and set them by a slow fire; they will produce a great deal of liquor, which you must strain; and put to it four ounces of shalots, two cloves of garlic, a good deal of pepper, ginger, mace, cloves, and a few bay leaves—boil and skim very well. When cold, cork close. In two months boil it up again with a little fresh spice and a stick of horse-radish, and it will then keep the year, which mushroom catsup rarely does, if not boiled a second time.

EEL SAUCE.—Cut the eels into large pieces and put them into a stewpan with a few slices of bacon, ham, veal, two onions, with all sorts of roots; soak it till it catches, then add a glass of white wine and good broth, a little cullis, three or four tarragon leaves, chervil, a clove of garlic, two spices and a bay leaf; simmer for an hour, skim it very well and sift in a sieve for use.

KIDNEY GRAVY.—*Time, an hour and three-quarters.*—Slice four kidneys, cut them into pieces, and dredge them with flour; put them into a stewpan with two ounces and a half of butter, a few sweet herbs and half an onion. Shake these over the fire for six or eight minutes, and then add about a pint of water. Let it simmer for an hour and three quarters, skimming it carefully; strain the gravy and set it by for use. This gravy can be made from one beef kidney, instead of four sheep's kidneys.

To PICKLE MUSHROOMS.—Take button mushrooms; rub and clean them with flannel and salt; throw some salt over them, and lay them in a stewpan with mace and pepper. While the liquor comes from them, keep shaking them well till the whole is dried into them again; then pour in as much vinegar as will cover them; warm them on the fire, and turn them into a jar. Mushrooms prepared in this manner are excellent, and will keep for two years.

PICKLED WALNUTS.—When they will bear a pin to go into them, place in a brine of salt and water boiled and strong enough to bear an egg on it, being quite cold first. It must be well skimmed while boiling. Let them soak six days, then change the brine; let them stand six more; then drain them and put them into a jar; pour over them a pickle of the best white wine-vinegar, with a good quantity of pepper, pimento, ginger, mace, cloves, mustard seeds and horseradish, all boiled together, but cold. To every hundred of walnuts put six spoonfuls of mustard seed and two or three heads of shalot. Keep them six months.

COMMON PUFF PASTE.—Put one pound of sifted flour on the slab, or in an earthen basin; make a hollow in the center, work into it a quarter of a pound of lard and half a teaspoonful of salt. When it is mixed through the flour, add as much cold water as will bind it together; then strew a little flour over the pasteboard or table; flour the rolling-pin, and roll out the paste to half an inch in thickness; divide half a pound of butter in three parts, spread one evenly over the paste, fold it up, dredge a little flour over it and the paste-slab, or table, roll it out again, spread another portion of the butter over it, roll it out again, and so continue until all the butter is used; roll it out to a quarter of an inch in thickness for use.

VERY RICH SHORT CRUST.—Break ten ounces of butter into a pound of flour, dried and sifted; add a pinch of salt and two ounces of loaf sugar rolled fine. Make it into a very smooth paste, as light as possible, with two well-beaten eggs, and sufficient milk to moisten the paste.

An Antidote for Tobacco.—Trask, the anti-tobacco philanthropist, says that gentian root coarsely ground, chewed well, and the saliva swallowed, will cure the appetite for tobacco, if its use is persisted in for a few weeks. Take as much of it after each meal, or oftener, as amounts to a common quid of "fine cut" or "cavendish."

Indelible Ink.—An excellent ink of this kind may be prepared by rubbing up one drachm of analine black with a mixture of sixty drops of concentrated hydrochloric acid, and one and one half ounce of alcohol. The resulting deep blue liquid is then to be diluted with a hot solution of one and one-half drachms of gum arabic in six ounces of water. This ink does not corrode a steel pen, and is affected neither by concentrated mineral acids nor by strong lye. If the analine black solution be diluted with one and one half ounces of shellac, dissolved in six ounces of alcohol, instead of with gum water, an analine black is obtained, which, after being applied to wood stained black, brass or leather, is remarkable for its extraordinary deep black color.

French Loaf Cake.—Two cups of white sugar, one scant cup of butter, one cup of sweet milk, three heaping cups of flour, three eggs, two teaspoonfuls cream of tartar, one teaspoonful soda. Put sugar, butter, eggs, (not previously beaten), soda, and cream of tartar all together, beat to a froth; add the milk, beating well, flavor with lemon extracts; add the flour gradually, pour into a cake-tin lined with buttered paper, sprinkle a little powdered sugar over the cake before baking. It is well to cover it when first putting in the oven, in order not to harden the top too soon.

Ginger Biscuits.—Eight ounces of flour, four ounces of butter, four ounces of loaf sugar; yolks of three eggs and some ground ginger.

Beat the butter to a cream before the fire, add the flour by degrees, then the sugar, pounded and sifted and a flavoring to taste of ground ginger, and mix the whole with the yolks of three well beaten eggs. When thoroughly mixed, drop the biscuit mixture on buttered paper, a sufficient distance from each other, to allow the biscuits to spread, and bake them a light color in a rather slow oven.

GOOSEBERRY TART.—Cut off the tops and tails from a quart of gooseberries; put them into a deep pie dish with five or six ounces of good moist sugar; line the edge of the dish with short crust; put on the cover, ornament the edges and top in the usual manner, and bake in a brisk oven. Serve with boiled custard, or a jug of cold cream.

FIG CAKE.—Two cups of sugar, one of butter, one of cold water, with a teaspoonful of soda dissolved in it; three cups of raisins, chopped fine, cinnamon and nutmeg, four eggs, one pound of figs; use the figs whole, covering them well with the cake to prevent burning. Bake in layers, frosting between each layer. Make as stiff as pound cake. Cut with a very sharp knife to prevent crumbling. This recipe makes two loaves.

BREAD PANCAKES.—*Time, five minutes.*—Soak pieces of stale bread in water until quite soft; drain through a sieve, then rub the bread through a colander. To a quart add three eggs and milk enough to make a soft batter.

COMMON PANCAKES.—*Time, five minutes.*—Beat three eggs, and stir them into a pint of milk; add a pinch of salt, and sufficient flour to make it into a thick, smooth batter; fry them in boiling fat, roll them over on each side, drain and serve them very hot, with lemon and sugar.

ARROWROOT FRITTERS.—Put two pints of milk, in a good sized stewpan, over the fire until it boils; have ten ounces of arrowroot ready mixed, and stir it into the milk as quickly as possible; add a little vanilla and yolks of eight eggs, the sugar the last. Stir it for about twenty minutes over a quick fire, then put it into a deep cutlet pan, and bake it about ten minutes in a quick oven. When it is quite cold, cut out the fritters with a round cutter, and egg and bread crumb them, glaze and send them up quite hot.

PICKLED PEACHES.—Nine pounds peaches, three pounds sugar, three quarts good cider vinegar. Peel the peaches, put two cloves in each peach, then put them with the sugar and vinegar in a porcelain lined kettle; cook from five to ten minutes. Add a little whole allspice.

CHICKEN SALAD.—Boil a chicken; do not chop very fine; cut up one bunch of celery, the size of a cent; to make the dressing, wash smooth the yolk of a hard-boiled egg, one teaspoonful of salt, one or two tablespoonfuls of made mustard; stir in slowly four tablespoonfuls of sweet oil, then two tablespoonfuls of vinegar; pour over the chicken and celery.

TO PICKLE CABBAGE.—Quarter them till they are thin enough to let the vinegar strike through; put them down in layers with spices, salt, and vinegar; scald your vinegar as often as is necessary to make them tender.

CRULLERS.—Six eggs, six tablespoonfuls powdered sugar, six tablespoonfuls melted butter, a wineglass of brandy, and a little nutmeg; flour as for doughnuts. Roll thin and cut into fanciful shapes with a jagging iron.

GELATINE FROSTING.—One teaspoonful gelatine, two tablespoonfuls of cold water; when the gelatine is soft, one tablespoonful of hot water. When entirely dissolved, add one cup of powdered sugar, and beat it while it is yet warm, until white and light; lemon to taste. This frosts one sheet of cake.

RASPBERRY JAM.—Allow a pound of sugar to each pound of fruit; press them with a spoon in an earthen dish, add the sugar, and boil all together for fifteen minutes.

BAVARIAN CREAM.—Dissolve half a package of gelatine in one quart of boiling milk; stir until it is dissolved, then add a pint of cream, and sweeten to taste. Add three tablespoonfuls of extract of vanilla. Let it cool a little, stirring it occasionally; then put it into custard cups, or in a mold, and leave it in a cold place till ready to use.

CANDIED FRUITS.—Preserve the fruit, then dip it in sugar boiled to candy thickness; afterwards dry it. Grapes may be thus dipped uncooked, and then dried. Or fruit may be taken from the syrup when preserved, rolled in powdered sugar, and afterwards set on a sieve to dry.

PLAIN PLUM CAKE.—Beat six ounces of butter to a cream, to which add six well-beaten eggs; work in one pound of flour, and half a pound of sifted loaf sugar, half a pound of currants, and two ounces of candied peels; mix well together, put it into a buttered tin, and bake it in a quick oven.

GINGER SNAPS.—Work a quarter of a pound of butter into a pound of fine flour, then mix it with a half pound of molasses, a quarter of a pound brown sugar, and one tablespoonful each of ginger and caraway seeds. Work it all well together, and form it into cakes not larger then a crown piece; place them on a baking tin in a moderate oven, when they will be dry and crisp.

HOMINY MUFFINS.—*Time, fifteen minutes.*—Take two cups of fine hominy, boiled and cold; beat it smooth; stir in three cups of sour milk, half a cup of melted butter, two teaspoonfuls of salt, and two tablespoonfuls of white sugar; then add three eggs well beaten, one teaspoonful of soda dissolved in hot water, and one large cup of flower; bake quickly.

FRIED BREAD.—*Time, ten minutes.*—Beat four eggs very light; add three tablespoonfuls of brown sugar, a little grated nutmeg, a tablespoonful of orange or rose water, and a quart of milk. Cut into slices, an inch thick, a stale loaf of bread; remove the crust from the sides, and cut each slice into halves. Butter your frying-pan, and when hot, lay in your bread (dipped in the custard), and brown on both sides. Lay them in a hot dish, and sprinkle over them a little loaf sugar.

SWEDISH JELLY.—Cover a knuckle of veal with water, add a small onion and a carrot, and let it boil until the meat is ready to fall off the bone. Take the meat and hash it fine, and return it to the liquor after it is strained, and give it another boil until it jellies. Add salt, pepper, the juice and rind of a lemon, cut fine, and then pour into a form. Put it into a cold place. It makes a nice dish for lunch or tea. If the knuckle of veal is large, use three quarts of water; if small, two quarts; let it boil slowly three or four hours, or until it is reduced to about half the quantity of water put in.

NEW ENGLAND PANCAKES.—Mix a pint of cream, five spoonfuls of fine flour, seven yolks and four whites of eggs, and a very little salt; fry them very thin in fresh butter, and between each strew sugar and cinnamon. Send up six or eight at once.

The 5 Cent
WIDE AWAKE LIBRARY.
—o—
The Best Stories by the Best Authors, Both Humorous and Sensational.
—o—
PRICE 5 CENTS A COPY.
—o—
READ THE LIST.

www.ingramcontent.com/pod-product-compliance
Lightning Source LLC
Chambersburg PA
CBHW032045090426
42733CB00030B/704